Illustrated HORSEWATCHING

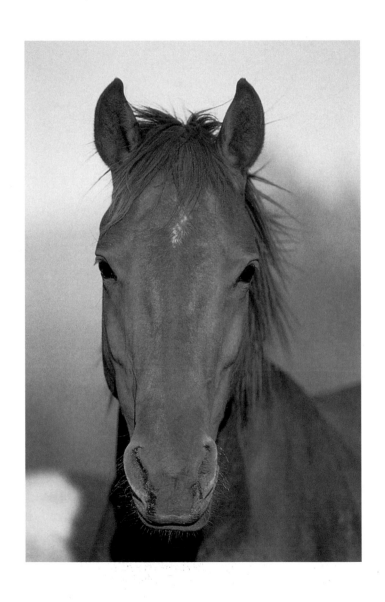

Illustrated Horsewatching

DESMOND MORRIS

EBURY
PRESS

First published in Great Britain by Jonathan Cape

This edition first published in 1997 by Ebury Press

1 3 5 7 9 10 8 6 4 2

Designed by David Fordham
Picture research by Nadine Bazar

Ebury Press
Random House, 20 Vauxhall Bridge Road,
London SW1V 2SA

Random House Australia Pty Limited
20 Alfred Street, Milsons Point, Sydney,
New South Wales 2061,
Australia

Random House New Zealand Limited
18 Poland Road, Glenfield, Auckland 10, New Zealand

Random House South Africa (Pty) Limited
PO Box 337, Bergvlei, South Africa

Random House UK Limited Reg. No. 954009

A CIP catalogue record for this book is available from the British Library

ISBN 0 09 1851513

Typeset by MATS, Southend-on-Sea, Essex
Printed by Tien Wah Press

CONTENTS

INTRODUCTION

IF THE DOG IS MAN'S BEST FRIEND, THEN THE HORSE could be well described as man's best slave. For thousands of years horses have been harnessed, ridden, spurred and whipped. They have been ruthlessly driven into the centre of bloody battlefields where they have been hacked to pieces. For centuries they have toiled to drag heavy loads in the service of human ambition and then been rewarded at the end of their days with a trip to the knacker's yard. Their endless exploitation has been due to their amazing willingness to cooperate with their human companions and to struggle as best they can to please us. This temperament, stems from their naturally sociable lifestyle in the wild. Horses are by nature herd animals that live in small bands where cooperation is as powerful a theme as competition and where affection for one another is so strong that it is easily transformed into a horse-human bond. Unfortunately for the horse, this bond ends with the human partner coming out on top, both literally and metaphorically. Being so good-natured has cost the horse dearly.

The other side of the coin is man's great love and respect for the horse, now stronger than ever. For every example of brutality there are many cases of human devotion to horses, shown in long hours of selfless care and protection. For every callous horse-whipper today there is an army of passionate horse-lovers, ready to rise at dawn and endure repeated hardships to ensure that their adored equines enjoy the best lifestyle possible. No animal is more admired or more highly valued.

What is it about the horse that awakens such intense feelings? Is it the animal's looks or its behaviour, its graceful athleticism or its personality? The answer is to be found in a remark made nearly four hundred years ago by the naturalist Edward Topsel when he wrote of the horse that it possesses 'a singular body and a noble spirit, the principal whereof is a loving and dutiful inclination to the service of Man, wherein he never faileth in Peace nor War . . . and therefore . . . we must needs account it the most noble and necessary creature of all four-footed Beasts.' The clue to its special appeal is summed up by the words 'noble and necessary'. It is the combination of its proud bearing with its slavish service to man that makes it so irresistible. If it were useful but ungainly, like a pig, or a cow, we would be grateful for its services but would not, perhaps, compose poems to it or wax lyrical about its great spirit. No, the secret of equine appeal is that it slaves for us while still looking noble. It is our humble servant even though it has the demeanour of an animal aristocrat. The mixture is magical. If such a dignified beast is subordinate to our will, then we must indeed be masters of the world.

So it was, from the very start of equine domestication, that man came under the spell of the horse. And right from the beginning there was one feature in particular that made a special impact on human affairs: its swift legs. Put to work for mankind, they gave a sudden boost to human expansion. For the first time our ancestors could move fast from place to place. Previously cattle had been the beasts of burden, the draught animals and the pullers of the plough. Now they could be restricted to the slower, clumsier tasks and the long-distance duties could be carried out more quickly by the horse. The mobility of man was magnified dramatically. Civilization could spread, trade routes could be opened up that were previously impossible. Cultural exchanges could be developed and the hybridization of ideas rapidly led to new creative vigour. For thousands of years, right up to the arrival of the internal combustion engine, the horse was the vehicle of the human conquest of the earth.

Its swift legs are significant, too, in having created its noble image. Because wild horses are fast-moving plains-living grazers, specialized for open country, they have had to evolve, over millions of years, the elegant frame of the muscle-rippling athlete. Rapid movement demands a certain style of body-structure, a style which we, as athletes ourselves, appreciate. As a species we are fast runners, too

– not diggers or climbers or clingers, but sprinters – and this gives us a common bond with the horse and a deeply rooted admiration for its amazing pace and grace. Psychologically it becomes an extension of our own running bodies. Sitting on its back we fuse with it in our minds to become one single, galloping, invincible being – the great centaur of ancient mythology.

When did all this happen? Surprisingly the horse was something of a late-comer on the domestic scene. Dogs, goats, sheep and cattle had all been brought under human control for thousands of years when in the third millennium B.C. the horse was first domesticated. This took place in the area which is now southern Russia and north-west Asia, as part of the advancing tide of agricultural management. It was not, of course, mankind's first contact with the horse. Horses had been hunted for food since the Old Stone Age, as the beautiful prehistoric paintings on the cave walls of France and Spain testify, but there was then no attempt to bring them under control. They were trapped, speared and eaten and that was the limit of our relationship with them.

An intriguing sideline on this hunting phase is the fact that the number of wild horses was already decreasing without any help from humans. This was because at the end of the Ice Age there was a rapid spread of thick forests

across most of the temperate zone. As an animal of the open plains, the horse was therefore losing ground little by little and it is estimated that it might well have become extinct eventually had the ancient farmers not intervened and domesticated the species before it vanished for ever. This is a pleasant reversal of the usual tale, in which human intervention condemns many a species to early retirement.

By the second millennium B.C. the decline of the horse had been turned around and as a domesticated animal it was once again spreading across Europe and increasing in numbers everywhere. By 1500 B.C. there were already two distinct types of domestic horse – the stocky ones of the colder northern regions and the slender ones in the warmer south. Specialization was beginning. From the heavy-set northern ponies, by selective breeding, came the giant breeds that were to be the great beasts of burden in the farmers' fields and on the soldiers' battlegrounds. From the leggy southern horses came the magnificent Arab steeds that were later to father the modern thoroughbreds of the racecourse. Wherever man explored and extended his range the horse went with him, until together they both acquired an almost global distribution. In the New World the Spanish intruders took a handful of horses with them – Columbus took thirty and Corte[ac]s sixteen – and before long these were to give

rise to a whole new population of 'Indian horses' and to change the social structure of the Plains Indians of the Americas.

As human populations everywhere began to explode into teeming millions, the numbers of horses thrown into service of these growing communities reached new heights. The whole of society seemed to be dependent on equine abilities, for farming, transportation, warfare, ceremony, sport and pleasure. As weapons became more advanced, the fate of horses in times of war became more hideous. In a single day's fighting during the First World War seven thousand horses were killed. Of the million British horses sent to the front in that most devastating conflict, only 62,000 were ever to see British soil again. The majority of those that were lucky enough to escape the bombs and shells were rewarded after the armistice by being fed to prisoners of war or sold to continental farmers to be converted into fertilizer.

Despite the helplessness of horses in the face of the new weaponry, there was one final cavalry charge at the start of the Second World War. In 1939 the Polish cavalry rode bravely into battle against the tanks and dive bombers of the Nazis. They were totally obliterated. The warhorse was gone for ever. We who watch war films today are spared the horrors of equine bloodshed. Trained film

horses are too valuable to be killed for our entertainment, so their demise is merely suggested and we easily forget what a terrible price we have made the obedient horse pay for its domestication by man.

With the coming of the industrial revolution the age of the horse began to wane. At first trains replaced the transportation horse, then motor-cars. Finally, mechanized equipment swamped them out, both on the road and in the field. Lorries, tractors, tanks, buses, coaches, vans and family cars took over. The blacksmith became an endangered species. Only nostalgia kept the working horse alive. Apart from racing and leisure-riding there was little for the modern horse to do. But with the removal of the arduous labour of earlier days came a growing respect and appreciation for our equine companions. Today, more than ever before, this respect is spreading with each generation. Equine commerce has been replaced by a much kinder equine love-affair. For the first time in five thousand years it is once again a good time to be a horse. Man's best slave may not have been completely freed to roam the plains but his slavery is now at least a benign one, full of care and devotion.

Back in the Elizabethan era, John Florio wrote, 'England is the paradise of women, the purgatory of men and the hell of horses.' Today that hell has become something approaching a heaven for most of our horses, as we start to repay our long-standing debt to the noble beast. But strangely, even in our most zealous and enthusiastic infatuation with the horse we still fail to appreciate it for its own sake, as a remarkable species full of subtle expressions, body language and social behaviour. It is possible to be an expert horseman or horse-woman and still not fully comprehend the nature of equine social life. The bond between horse and rider dominates to the exclusion of horse-to-horse relations. *Horsewatching* fills this gap with some objective observations of one of our closest animal allies. And it ends with an examination of some of the less familiar aspects of horse myths and folklore. It is a book for horse-watchers everywhere, whether they have spent fifty years in the saddle or have never encountered a horse outside their television screens. After reading it, I hope you will agree that the horse is, even today, a 'noble and necessary' creature that enriches all our lives merely by its presence among us.

WHAT DOES A HORSE SIGNAL WITH ITS EARS?

THE EARS OF A HORSE ARE SELDOM STILL. LIKE RADAR dishes scanning the skies, they are forever moving this way and that, picking up tiny sound clues from the world around them. For the wild ancestors of the domestic horse this was particularly important trait. Their only method of self-protection was fast retreat from danger and it was vital that they should be aware of the very first signs of trouble so that they could take off at high speed in the split second before a predator could leap to the attack. Their mobile ears were their only early warning system.

Because the position of the ears varies as the horse's mood changes, its ear postures can be read as signals by its companions. One horse can tell the emotional condition of another by glancing at the way its ears are held or moved. So the ears have a double role – they receive sound signals and they transmit visual signals. The visual signals are unusually helpful because equine ears are so conspicuous. Other hooved animals, such as cattle, antelope and deer, have horns or antlers protruding from the tops of their heads, which tend to hide their ear movements. But the ears of horses, not being obscured in this way, are highly visible even from a considerable distance, or when the animal can only be seen in silhouette. The language of equine ears is as follows.

When the ears are neutral they are held loosely upwards, with their openings pointing forward and outwards. In this way they scan the area in front of the horse and to either side of it. This basic posture provides the best coverage of the environment, but the moment a strange sound is heard, one or both ears rotate instantly to face it and examine it more carefully.

If a sound appears to be strange or worrying, the horse also turns its head or even its whole body towards the source and then pricks its ears so they are stiffly erect with their apertures facing directly towards the sound. *Pricked ears* are typical of horses that are startled, vigilant, alert or merely interested and are most commonly seen during frontal greetings.

The opposite of pricked ears are *airplane ears*. Here they flop out laterally with their openings facing down towards the ground. These are the ears of a tired or lethargic horse or one that has completely lost interest in the world around it – they indicate clearly that the animal is psychologically at a low ebb. Sometimes the posture becomes more extreme and there is a *drooped ears* posture, with the ears hanging down loosely on either side of the head. This is seen when a horse becomes very dozy or is in actual pain and wants to switch off all incoming messages. These sideways ear postures are also used as

signals of inferiority during status battles or stressful social encounters. The weak horse is saying, 'I am not arguing with you, I have switched off, you are the boss, so now leave me alone.'

Sometimes it is possible to observe a ridden horse adopting *drooped backwards ears* as a special signal. The ears are stuck out sideways, but their openings are directed backwards towards the rider. This indicates a horse that is submissive towards and fearful of its human companion. The lateral element of the ear posture reveals the submissiveness and the twisting backwards of the apertures shows the animal's need to catch any tiny sound from the fear-inducing figure on its back. This ear posture is common in horses with brutal owners. It is also observed when male and female horses encounter one another in a sexual mood. The female often adopts this position of the ears when her strong sexual urges make her approach a powerful stallion. She is attracted to him, but at the same time is rather fearful of him and signals this with her ears. For him, the submissiveness of her ear signals acts as a positive sexual stimulant and reassures him that he is not about to be dealt a savage kick as he approaches her from behind.

If ordinary fear turns to blind panic, alert ears return. They are more erect now but at the same time they are busily twitching and flicking. A horse with *flicking ears* may well be on the verge of bolting in terror.

At the opposite end of the emotional scale, where anger, aggression and dominance rear their heads, there is the characteristic *pinned ears* signal in which the horse flattens its ears back against its head so that they almost disappear from view. In silhouette, an angry horse looks quite earless and it has been suggested that one of the reasons why humans can control horses so easily is that we must always appear dominant and ferocious to them simply because our own ears are for ever pinned to the sides of our heads. In horse language this must make us seem very intimidating indeed, and there is nothing they can do – it must seem to them – to change our domineering mood. No matter how submissively they behave, we never prick up our ears in a greeting, or flop them out sideways in dozy subordination.

There is a good reason for the pinned ear signal being the most aggressive. It is derived from the primeval horse's 'ear-protection' posture employed to keep ears as safe as possible from the attacks of rivals. Tucked back they are least likely to be bitten or torn, and during the course of evolution that old self-defence posture has become part of everyday equine body language. Instead of being reserved purely for moments of actual fighting, it is now employed

as a threat signal when two rival horses encounter one another. The aggressive animal simply pins back its ears, saying in effect, 'If you want a fight I am ready for one,' and the other horse can then either act submissively or threaten back. In this way disputes can often be settled without recourse to serious fighting, these displays usefully replacing the bites and kicks that both animals would prefer to avoid.

In one special context there are two unusual ear reactions. If a racehorse is drugged, its condition is most clearly revealed by the odd way in which its ears behave. If it has been given a depressant, its ears droop out sideways and do so even when it is otherwise active. When it walks these drooping ears may flop up and down, as though they are no longer being operated by the ear muscles. If the drugged horse has, on the other hand, been given stimulants, its ears then go completely rigid. In these two situations it is possible to have one's suspicions aroused when a particular horse behaves oddly before a race.

Finally, it must always be remembered that during a horse's daily life, its ears (in normal, undrugged animals) are constantly moving to pick up new sounds. Mobile ears, turning this way and that, are, by their very activity, signals of shifting attention and interest. Companion horses can quickly note the way in which another member of the herd has become curious about something in the distance. Then they too can home in with their listening devices. These shifts in direction can override other considerations. If a noise is coming from behind, the ears will be rotated backwards regardless of the general mood of the animal. Only when these listening actions have died down will the ears revert to their quieter, long-term 'mood posture'. Horses are quick to learn the differences between short-term attention signals and long-term mood signals, and it is easy enough for us to do the same. Once we have learnt this simple 'language' of the equine ears it will help us to tell at a glance the emotional state of our animals and allow us to enter their world more intimately.

HOW WELL CAN HORSES HEAR?

BETTER THAN WE CAN. THEIR HIGHLY SENSITIVE EARS can detect a wider range of sounds, from very low frequency to very high, and at all levels they have more acute hearing.

Adult humans have the ability to hear sounds up to about 20,000 cycles per second but this sinks to 12,000 by the time we are in our sixties. Tests on horses have established that they can hear up to 25,000 cycles, appreciably above our range, but as with us this starts to decline with age. The acuity of their hearing exceeds ours thanks to their large and wonderfully mobile external ears. Controlled by no fewer than sixteen muscles, each ear can be rotated through about 180 degrees, pinpointing the source of particular sounds from a great distance. Time and again a horse-owner has noticed that his horse has reacted to an approaching noise before he himself could detect anything.

Horses are so good at detecting natural disturbances such as distant storms, high winds and earthquakes that some horsemen have insisted that their animals possess a sixth sense. To be certain of this, however, it would be necessary to study the reactions of a totally deaf horse. The chances are that in all such 'mysterious' reactions the horses are in reality responding to tiny sounds that are still too far away for the human ear. Even earthquakes may be sensed in this way because they are preceded by low frequency geophysical vibrations that could be heard at the lower end of a horse's hearing range. People living in earthquake zones have frequently noted that their steeds become intensely agitated and highly vocal just before a quake strikes – a useful early warning for insensitive humans.

These comments should not be taken to mean that horses necessarily lack a sixth sense, but merely that we should be wary of assuming that such a sense is operating if we observe an equine reaction that is inexplicable to us. However, it is possible that if we could eliminate all the normal senses of sound, sight, smell, taste and touch, we might well find that, like many other species, the horse is able to respond to such clues as the changing magnetic field of the earth. Many riders, thrown by their horses during an afternoon ride, have marvelled at the way their animals have unerringly found their way back home, over strange terrain, later that night. Such cases may be examples of sensitive hearing – the twisting ears of the animal picking up distant, familiar sounds – or they may be examples of even more extraordinary sensitivity to the 'magnetic map' of the home territory. Whichever sense is operating, one thing is certain . . . horses are remarkably finely tuned to the environment in which they live.

Such is this sensitivity that a particularly noisy environment can be distressing to a horse. People who keep their animals near to airports or busy road systems report that they often become highly strung. What for us would be an unpleasant cacophony of sounds must rise to an unbearable din for the horses. They can shut out the sounds to some extent by flattening their ears, but even this is not enough and care should be taken to avoid such locations wherever possible. Police and parade horses have to be schooled into the highly unnatural response of *not* reacting to shouts, cheers, drums and bands on public or ceremonial occasions and this requires a great deal of patience and training. Even when they have had their natural reactions suppressed in this way they can be observed, on the great day, to wince and twitch as the blasts of sound hit them. They may not rear up or flee in panic as they wish to do, but they still show by their telltale body-language that they are far from calm as their delicate ears are bombarded with painful stimuli.

One special benefit of the horse's sensitivity to sound is that an intelligent rider can readily train a horse to respond to softly spoken, simple words of command. Any horse can be made to react, just like a dog, to words such as 'stop', 'go', 'yes' and 'no' – and many others – but for some reason this ability is not utilized to the full. Some horsemen seem to feel, misguidedly, that it is wrong to talk to a horse and that all commands should be given by physical means – tugging, pulling, twisting and the rest – but such an attitude fails to make use of one of the horse's great attributes – its brilliant sense of hearing.

HOW MANY SOUNDS DOES A HORSE MAKE?

THE VOCAL REPERTOIRE OF THE HORSE IS NOT GREAT and the sounds it can make are far from musical, but it nevertheless possesses a simple, useful language of snorts and squeals, neighs and nickers, which convey its changing moods to its companions. There are eight main sounds:

1 THE SNORT

This carries the message 'There may be danger here.' It is performed by a horse experiencing a conflict between curiosity and fear. It detects something that arouses its interest, but which makes it slightly wary, and the snorting reaction does two things simultaneously: it clears the animal's respiratory passage, ready for action, and it also alerts the other members of the herd to the possibility of danger. Because the snorting horse faces the possible threat, the sound acts as an indicator of the direction from which the threat is coming, allowing the other horses to focus on it as well. In a sense it is the equine equivalent to the much louder canine bark. The snorting horse, unlike the barking dog, can only be heard from a distance of about 50 yards. This means that if it has spotted something worrying in the far distance, it can alert its companions without revealing the presence of the herd to what may be a prowling predator.

The snort is a powerful exhalation of air through the nose, with the mouth held shut. It lasts between 0.8 and 0.9 of a second and has an audible fluttering pulse created by the vibrations of the nostrils. The head is usually held high, as is the tail, with the whole body of the horse showing a state of high excitement and readiness for fleeing.

Although its most common use is when a strange object is detected in the distance, it is also frequently employed when one stallion challenges another. Again the mood is one of great interest tinged with anxiety – a state of conflict.

2 THE SQUEAL

This is a defensive signal. In aggressive encounters it means 'Don't push me any further' and suggests to the rival that if it fails to desist, retaliation will be provoked. A lactating mare that has sore nipples and resents being touched will also squeal as a protest. And a flirting mare being approached by a stallion will object to his advances with this same sound. In all cases, the squeal acts as a protest signal, saying, 'Stop it!', but in sexual encounters it sometimes has an added nuance, the message then being 'Stop it, I like it!'

Squeals vary considerably in intensity. They may be as short as 0.1 of a second, or as long as 1.7 seconds. At full

strength they may be heard up to 100 yards away. Some of the loudest squeals are heard during encounters between stallions and mares. Squealing is usually performed with a closed mouth, but sometimes the corners of the mouth may open slightly.

3 THE GREETING NICKER

This is a low-pitched, gutteral sound with a pulsating quality that is employed as a friendly 'come here' signal. It is used at close quarters, once the companion has been recognized, and can be heard at a distance of up to 30 yards. It is given when one horse greets another one in a welcoming fashion and it is also commonly heard at the horses's feeding time, when it is given to the human companion bringing them their food. In such cases it has been called a 'begging' sound, but it is really more of a general salutation – the horse is saying in effect, 'Hello, good to see you!'

4 THE COURTSHIP NICKER

Performed by a stallion approaching a mare, this is also a greeting, but it carries with it specifically sexual flavour to rouse the interest of the female. The human equivalent would be something like a flirtatious 'Hello, beautiful!' As the stallion performs this nicker, he often nods his head vigorously, keeping the mouth shut and the nostrils wide open. This kind of nicker is longer, lower and more broken up into syllables. Different stallions have different pulse rates in their courtship nickers, so that it should be possible for the female to identify the approaching male without even looking at him.

5 THE MATERNAL NICKER

This is given by a mare to her foal and is very soft, barely audible from a distance. It is used when the mare is mildly concerned about her offspring's safety and the gentle, intimate message is 'Come a little closer.' Foals react to this sound from birth, without any learning process. In fact, it is possible to get a newborn foal to follow a human simply by imitating this sound, so compulsive is their response to it.

6 THE NEIGH

Sometimes called the whinny, this sound starts out as a squeal and then ends as a nicker. It is the longest and loudest of horse calls, lasting an average of 1.5 seconds and being audible over half a mile away. This is the equine equivalent of the canine howl, given when one horse becomes isolated from its group, or when it spots one of its companions in the distance. Usually the call is answered, the messages being something like 'I am over here, is that you?' and 'Yes, it's me, I hear you.' It helps to keep a group together or at least to maintain contact at a distance. Experiments have revealed that horses react more strongly to the neighing of members of their own groups than to strange horses. And mares are more responsive to their own foals than to other young horses. This proves that each neigh is learned as a means of personal identification. Listening closely to different neighs, it soon becomes clear that they do in fact each have their own special quality. There are even breed differences in addition to individual ones. And it is possible to tell a male neigh from a female one by the little grunt that stallions add at the end of their calls. Some people believe that neighing or whinnying is a sign of fear and panic, but this is a complete misunderstanding. It is a request for information, not a cry of alarm.

7 THE ROAR

When horses are fighting seriously and are in a savagely emotional mood – it may be intense fear, intense rage, or both at once – they can be heard to roar or, at a higher pitch, to scream. These sounds are rarely heard in domestic horses unless they are running wild in a natural herd or are being kept in a large breeding group – not a common occurrence where modern horse management is concerned.

8 THE BLOW

This is like a snort without the pulsations or fluttering quality in the noise. It is a simple exhalation of air through the nose and carries a similar message to the snort, but

with less tension. The blow may say, 'What's this?' but sometimes it appears to be simply a signal of well-being, saying no more than 'Life is good!'

In addition, horses may be heard to grunt and groan with exertion or boredom, sigh occasionally and snore loudly, but these are of minor significance in their vocal repertoire. In truth, the horse does not have a very elaborate language of sounds and does not use them in a rigid manner. Not one of them is confined to a single context with a single message. Although 'typical' messages have been given here, each sound can be heard in a whole variety of situations, where other elements of the social event alter its precise meaning. Equine vocalizations should always be 'read' with this in mind.

WHAT DOES A HORSE SIGNAL WITH ITS TAIL?

A HORSE'S TAIL RISES AND FALLS LIKE A NEEDLE ON A dial that registers excitement. A tail held high signifies alertness, activity and exuberance. One drooped low indicates sleepiness, exhaustion, pain, intense fear or submission.

The reason for this is that the faster the horse accelerates as it moves forwards, the more its 'anti-gravity' muscle system goes into action. These muscles help to lift it up and along, and the raising of the tail is part of this process. When the horse decelerates, putting on the brakes, the reverse occurs and the tail is pressed low. These ancient connections between up-and-go and down-and-stop have been 'borrowed' to provide special signals for equine body language. A horse may raise or lower its tail purely as a signal now, without even moving its body.

A boisterous young horse, for example, may approach another and show its readiness for play by flicking its tail high up over its back – as fully raised as is anatomically possible. Sometimes the tail may even curl right over its back, so intense is the 'lift' when initiating play. This invitation signal is immediately understood by another young horse and a game quickly begins. The key point here is that, at the moment of tail-raising, the animal inviting play may not have been accelerating. It may even have been stationary. Up-and-go has here been transformed into up-and-'let's go'. The movement of the tail is no longer *caused* by acceleration, it has become symbolic of it. It has become, as it were, a request for acceleration: 'Let's dash off and play together.'

In a similar way, a tail can be drooped by a stationary horse as a signal saying, 'I am tired and weak, I submit to you, you are the boss.' If acutely afraid of another horse, an animal may even tuck its tail tight against its rear end, almost like a dog trying to 'put its tail between its legs'.

If a horse becomes very aggressive or tense then another tail signal is a stiffening of the fleshy base of the tail, so that it tends to stick out behind the animal more than usual, as if it were a hairy rod.

In sexual encounters, the tails of both stallions and mares are held high because of the excitement of the moment, but there is a small difference, namely that the female's tail is also held over to one side as a sexual invitation signal, while it is kept in the raised posture.

In addition to the up-and-down signals of the tail, there are also rapid swishing movements, in various directions. These are derived from irritation responses when a horse is troubled by insects and other pests. The tail in this context is being used essentially as a fly-switch, but equine body language has borrowed this primeval action, as it has others, for use in social encounters. An anxious,

frustrated or confused horse may flick its tail this way and that, first sideways, then vertically, then round in an arc, signalling its irritation. The 'fly' at which its tail is swishing has become symbolic. The source of the annoyance is now psychological rather than physical. In dressage contests this tail-wagging can cause a loss of points for what is termed 'resistance' – in other words it is taken as a sign that the horse is ill at ease and therefore badly prepared by its rider.

When a horse becomes particularly angry, it may express its mood by increasing the power of the tail-swish, delivering a side-flick so strong that the tail-hairs actually whistle through the air and can even draw blood if they strike human flesh. Or it may flick its tail high in the air and then slap it down hard. Clues such as these often herald a savage kick, as the horse's bad temper grows.

In some countries the illegal use of a whip equipped to give an electric shock produces a highly characteristic tail reaction. As the horse is 'buzzed' it stiffens the base of its tail, swings the tail round in a rapid circle, then lifts it high in the air and slaps it hard down on its rear end. This is all done in the space of a second, but it is a vital tell-tale clue that an illegal piece of goading has taken place.

Another bizarre form of cheating has been uncovered in the case of the high-stepping Tennessee Walkers. These often brutalized horses may have their tails docked and then false tails fitted over the stumps in an exaggeratedly erect posture, to give them that excited, high-tail look. Sometimes a piece of ginger is inserted in the unfortunate horse's anus, to also produce a similar effect. That old expression from countless Western movies – 'Let's hightail it out of here' – has somehow lost its innocence.

WHAT DOES A HORSE SIGNAL WITH ITS NECK?

THE HORSE'S LONG AND POWERFUL NECK GIVES IT THE ability to move its head about with considerable flexibility. This provides it with a variety of head and neck signals that can operate as useful clues to its many changing moods. Some of these actions are derived from cleaning movements. Horses suffer terribly from flies and other insect pests that buzz around their faces and neck and they frequently make a short sharp movement of the neck as a way of disturbing and possibly driving away these small tormenters. The most popular version is the *head shake*, a vigorous sideways action that can quickly shake up a cloud of flies. Another is the upward *head toss* and a third is the up-and-back movement of the *head jerk*. The primary role of these actions may be seen to be self-comforting, but they also exist in a secondary, social form. Whenever a horse is irritated by the actions of a companion, be it equine or human, it is likely to reveal its frustration and annoyance by behaving as though it is being tormented by insect pests. Tossing, shaking or jerking its head, it signals its annoyance even in the complete absence of any real insects. This is the equine equivalent of a human scratching the back of his head when he is feeling angry. Like horses, we perform a primitive 'irritation reaction' to a new form of irritation that is now completely in the mind. The people who infuriate us are not actually stinging the skin on top of our heads and yet we behave as if they are.

These tossing and shaking actions must not be confused with *head bobbing* in which the horse ducks the head down and back repeatedly. This is usually the animal's way of increasing its range of vision and improving its understanding of objects directly in front of it. The *head wobble* is another head movement with a very distinct meaning. In this, the nosetip of the head is twisted from side to side while the top of the head stays still. It is as if the animal is clearing its head, and its message is 'I am ready for action.' In a curious way it is almost self-congratulatory and there is a 'cocky' head sway seen among humans that has both a similar form and a similar meaning.

Forward movements of the head, such as *head thrusting*, *head lungeing* and *nose nudging* are all self-assertive actions. The thrust and the lunge are aggressive movements related to biting, but the nudge, performed with the top of the nose and with the mouth closed, is a milder display and says little more than 'Hey, what about me?' or 'Come on, let's get on with it.' It demands attention and is used both to horse and human companions. Sometimes it is used to gain interest when a horse is in acute discomfort and is an action that should never be ignored if the cause of it is not fully understood.

level of a real fight, with displays giving way to violent physical action, but this is always a last resort.

One of the reasons why there are so many 'objections' and 'steward's inquiries' at racetracks is because if a jockey urges his mount to shoulder barge a rival horse, the latter is not merely impeded but also psychologically intimidated, responding to it as though it is the gesture of an aggressive, dominant animal. This has the effect of slowing it up more than might be expected from the simple 'bumping' it receives. On the polo field, the same action is employed as an accepted element of the sport, a good polo pony being the one that is ready and willing to shoulder barge all-comers and never to be intimidated by such contacts.

The rump presentation is employed as a defensive display. The horse in question simply swings round so that its rump is offered to its rival. This is a more guarded form of threat and says, 'Stop annoying me or I will kick you.' In origin it is a lining-up of the body for a backwards kick and acts as a warning sign of a possible attack to come, should the other horse not keep its distance. In behaviour terms it is what is called an 'intention movement', because with it the animal signals its intention of making a vigorous action. Other horses quickly learn to read the preparatory stages of the action and respond to them without waiting for the rest of the movement to follow. In this way a rump display becomes an efficient substitute for a full rear-kicking action.

VII

WHAT DOES A HORSE SIGNAL WITH ITS LEGS?

THERE ARE SEVERAL LEG SIGNALS USED BY HORSES TO show their changing moods. One is *pawing the ground*. This is a scraping action of one front leg in which the foot is dragged backwards. In origin it is a feeding movement or a way of investigating the ground beneath the feet. It may be used to scratch beneath the surface or to test its resistance. On such occasions it is purely mechanical and does not act as part of equine body language, but it may also be employed emotionally in a non-mechanical way by frustrated horses that have a strong urge to move forwards. If something prevents them from advancing – either a fear of doing so or a physical obstruction – then they may start to paw at the ground as a way of expressing their thwarted feelings.

The *front-leg lift* is a threat. It is a mild version of the forward strike employed when horses attack one another frontally. If two stallions are doing battle they may both rear up on their hind legs and strike out with their front legs. The leg-lift is simply a way of saying, 'This is what I will do to you if you provoke me further,' and is the equine equivalent of the human fist-shake.

The *back-leg lift* is a more defensive threat acting as a signal that a full-blooded kick is on the way if matters get worse. It is used to amplify the rump-presentation signal if that has failed to have the desired effect. It is sometimes employed by mares that wish to repel their over-attentive foals. If the foals are being a nuisance and persist in searching for the udder at times when the mare does not want to feed them, she will drive them away with a firm lift of whichever hind leg is nearer to them.

Knocking and *stamping* are two other ways in which horses can signal to others that they are in a mildly threatening mood. Again, both actions are related to kicking, but in a highly modified form. Knocking consists of a raising and lowering of a hind-leg in such a way that it makes a forcible tapping sound on the ground. Stamping is a similar up-and-down movement performed with one of the front feet. Knocking and stamping are used in contexts that can best be described as 'mild protest'. A mare may knock when her foal is irritating her. A riding horse may stamp as a protest when it is being saddled up for a journey it does not want to make. Like many other body signals, these actions are directed not only towards other horses but also at human companions, who – consciously or unconsciously – soon learn to read the signs if they are to become good masters.

VIII

HOW EXPRESSIVE IS A HORSE'S FACE?

THE SUBTLE AND COMPLEX BODY LANGUAGE OF THE horse involves various facial expressions, not as elaborate as those of human beings but still able to convey many shifting moods and emotions.

The earliest expression seen in a young foal is one called 'snapping'. In this the animal opens its mouth, draws back its mouth-corners and then, with teeth exposed, starts to open and shut its jaws. Sometimes the teeth make contact and sometimes they just fail to do so. When they do snap together there is a clapping noise – some authors have called this action 'teeth-clapping'. Others have stressed the opening and closing of the jaws and have christened it 'jaw-waving'. Its function is submissive and the message is 'I am only a little foal and I mean you no harm so please don't hurt me.' It is performed towards any large or strange horse that comes close. By the time the young horses are three years old the action has almost ceased and its role in equine social life is clearly to protect the weak newcomers to the herd.

The curious feature of snapping is that at first glance it looks as though it is slightly aggressive – as if the young animal is making biting movements. But the older horses do not make this human error in interpretation, and they respond to it for what it is in horse language – a stylized grooming signal. When two horses meet they often express their friendliness by mutual grooming – each nibbling the other's mane or some other part of the coat. Such mutual aid is only possible when there is no tension or threat between the two animals. Making a movement as if to start grooming therefore has about it a highly non-aggressive flavour. The young foal, by making a mock-grooming movement with its mouth, is able to say in horse language, 'I am friendly,' and in that way escape any hostility from adults.

The exact opposite of this snapping mouth is when the jaws are held tensely open with the teeth fully exposed. This is the true bite-threat used in fighting as a warning of an imminent attack. It is often enough to see off an opponent without actual contact being made. At a less violent moment, a horse's tense aggression is shown by a tight-lipped mouth. Other forms of tension, such as fear, anxiety and pain, are also accompanied by a stiff mouth, in contrast with the relaxed lips of a peaceful animal or one that is exhausted. When a horse is sleepy it often lets its lower lip droop and sag down.

When sexually active, a stallion often shows the strange expression that is known as the 'flehmen face'. He does this in response to the smell of the mare's urine, curling up his top lip to expose the upper teeth and gums. He stretches his head forwards as he does this and appears to be sniffing

HOW WELL CAN HORSES SEE?

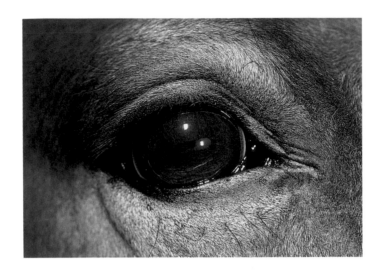

THE STRANGEST FEATURE OF THE HORSE'S EYE IS ITS huge size – twice as big as the human eye. It is one of the largest in the entire animal kingdom and amazingly is bigger than the eye of either the elephant or the whale. It also possesses a special light-intensifying device – the *tapetum lucidum* – which is a layer that reflects light back on to the retina and makes the horse much better than its rider at seeing in dim light. It also gives the horse's eye a 'glow' similar to the shine of a cat's eyes on dark nights.

Together these two facts – huge eyes with light-reflecting layers – lead to an inescapable conclusion: the horse is a nocturnal animal! To anyone who has studied zebra in the wild this will come as no great surprise, for herds of zebra are intensely active in very dim light at dawn and dusk and can obviously see much better than human beings in those conditions. But we are so used to thinking of the domestic horse as a daytime steed that we have overlooked this important aspect of its natural lifestyle. Riders who have risked jumping with their horses on moonlit nights report that, although it may be a nerve-racking experience for the human involved, the equine partner takes it all literally in his stride.

The fact that the horse is naturally active by night does not mean that it is naturally inactive by day. It is even more active by day and is in fact both strongly diurnal *and* nocturnal. Throughout the long waking phases of the day and night, the horse's eye is for ever scanning the horizon on the lookout for the threat of possible killers. And the eye is beautifully designed to be super-sensitive to tiny movements in the distance that would not be apparent to the human eye. Even today, after living its whole life in a completely lion-free world, a domestic horse can still be panicked by the sudden fluttering of a sheet of paper in the wind, somewhere at the edge of its range of vision. The old fears die hard.

Helping it in this vigil is its huge range of vision. A horse can see about 340 of the 360 degrees around it, with only two small blind spots, just in front and immediately behind its body. For this reason it is crucial not to approach a horse, even a normally docile one, from those angles. Its sudden realization that someone has come close to it, when an invisible hand pats or strokes it, may startle it badly. Always approach a horse from slightly to one side, where it can see you clearly.

Because the eyes of the horse are set on either side of its head, it does not normally see objects in depth, with binocular vision. It sees them flat, as we do if we shut one eye. It also sees less detail than we do, but is much more sensitive to movement than we are.

HOW DO HORSES FEED?

THIS MAY SEEM A SIMPLE QUESTION, BUT IT IS SURPRISING how much misunderstanding there is about equine feeding behaviour. Hardly any domestic horses are allowed to feed naturally and the results are often unpleasant. To understand what has gone wrong it helps to study the unrestricted feeding actions of rough-living, feral horses.

The first startling fact to emerge is that, given complete freedom, horses spend as much as sixteen hours a day feeding. Intrepid field observers have discovered that they even keep eating in the dark – as late as midnight – and then start up again in the early hours of the morning. The feeding is slow and selective, the horses working away at the vegetation with their amazingly active and mobile lips, sifting and choosing just the plants they want and pushing the others to one side with great dexterity. They seek variety. Although grasses are their main food, they also eat flowers, fruits, berries and nuts when the mood takes them. If they find themselves near water they gorge on aquatic plants. If the land is bare they will paw the ground digging up roots. If the grass is low they will switch to browsing on leaves. In other words, given free choice, they eat a varied and interesting herbivorous diet.

They eat much more slowly than cattle, for a good reason. Horses have comparatively small stomachs and unlike cows they each have only one stomach. Cows eat for about eight hours a day, munching and swallowing quickly, then spend a total of eight more hours chewing the cud – bringing wadges of undigested food back up into their mouths for prolonged grinding. Horses nibble, chew, swallow and then digest, little by little. They are uncomfortable if their small stomachs are empty, so they can hardly ever relax.

One mystifying feature of equine feeding is that horses can never vomit. They are simply incapable of it, having special one-way valves that prevent the food in their stomachs being 'thrown up'. For this reason they have to be especially careful and cautious in selecting their food plants because if they did consume something poisonous they could not cure themselves by being sick. Nobody knows why this shortcoming should exist in horse anatomy, but exist it does and makes feeding a risky business if there are many poisonous plants or other noxious substances in their environment.

Given that the natural feeding behaviour of horses involves endless, varied grazing, how does the feeding routine of the stabled horse compare with the free-roaming animal? Badly, is the short answer. In stables, horses are usually given only three feeds a day – rather like people – and the rest of the time they have to stand

around and occupy themselves with something else. This does not mean that they are nutritionally underfed. The fodder they are given is concentrated and of high quality. But it does mean that they are behaviourally underfed, and the consequences are well known. The stabled horse fed artificially in this way is liable to develop what are unfairly referred to as 'vices'.

The most common stable vices are crib-chewing, wind-sucking, lip-smacking, tongue-swallowing, dung-eating, bed-eating and rug-chewing. All of these are actions that the horses perform to relieve the endless boredom of simply standing still in a sterile little stable, and more specifically to replace the missing grazing actions. It does not make sense to give a horse all the nutrients it needs quickly, since each animal has a genetically programmed 'grazing-time' of at least twelve hours a day, and preferably sixteen hours, which it wants to fill with feeding activity, regardless of whether it has had the appropriate food intake or not. The horse is essentially a *low*-grade food specialist. It is programmed to spend ages consuming low-grade nutrients with plenty of fibre and bulk. To give horses high-grade food that they can eat rapidly goes against their basic nature. For many of them the outcome is 'vacuum eating' – chewing at the crib, nibbling at the wood of the stable doors, swallowing air that distends the stomach and makes

it feel full even when it is not, and eating dung that gives at least a little variety to the diet by adding a new flavour.

Fortunately these vices do not occur in the majority of stabled animals, although they can be found somewhere in almost every equine establishment. Somehow most high-grade-fodder horses manage to adapt to their unnatural regime. Their urge to go on and on grazing all day is still there, but it is suppressed. It may show itself in unusual ways – as when a particular horse becomes a 'bad-doer' or is 'temperamental and highly-strung'. Many of the problems of stabled horses, although seemingly remote from feeding problems, are in reality traceable back to the artificiality of modern feeding routines. But horses are such amenable creatures and they do their best to adjust to the bizarre human habit of having only three square meals a day. Perhaps it is just as well they do because if they did have free access to food they would put on weight dramatically and begin to develop the silhouette of round-bellied zebras, rather than sleekly elegant steeds. For under natural conditions horses would face bad periods each year – freezing cold in the northern climates every winter, when even sixteen hours of feeding a day would not result in much actual food intake, and searing drought in the warmer regions, where the feeding would involve many hours of arduous scraping with pawing hooves and

HOW DOES A MARE
DEAL WITH HER NEWBORN FOAL?

AS SHE COMES TO THE END OF HER PREGNANCY, THE mare shows signs of restlessness, a clear indication that birth is imminent. This unease is not simply a matter of bodily discomfort – it also reflects a special state of mind. The mare experiences a mood of anxiety, and there is a very good reason for this. She is about to become vulnerable – more vulnerable than she will ever be at any other time in her life. This may be no great hazard for a much loved and well tended domestic horse, but it is her ancient ancestry that speaks to her now, telling her to take care in her impending moment of almost complete helplessness. For a hungry predator in the wild, a mare giving birth to a foal is easy pickings, and precautions are necessary.

The mare has evolved a remarkable mechanism, not clearly understood, by which she is able to control the timing of the birth so that she is alone and in the dark. More than 90 per cent of all equine births take place in the middle of the night, and if the mare is part of a natural herd the birth takes place away from the other animals. Intriguingly, the mare will, if possible, seek out some damp or marshy land as a place to drop her foal, as if something about wet ground has a special advantage at this time. In domestic horses living in a field with a pond this has been known to lead to the drowning of the foal, the unfortunate newborn being deposited straight in the water. But in the wild this curious attraction to wet places may well have a more useful role, ensuring that the mare is close to a place where drinking will pose no problems during her vulnerable phase. Alternatively, the marshy areas may offer better cover for the young animal and may simply reflect a search for some kind of natural camouflage.

One consequence of the mare's urge to be alone at birth is that the presence of eager human companions, all too ready to give rarely needed assistance, is very disturbing to her. The mare has a special way of dealing with such intrusions. She waits. She controls her contractions and bides her time. Eventually the nocturnal vigil is relaxed and the watchers retire briefly for a warming drink. No sooner have they departed than she drops the foal. Many horse-owners who return to find a new foal tottering to its feet believe that it is simply bad luck that they have missed the great moment, but if they compared notes with other owners they would soon realize that it was not a matter of luck, but of the Garbo-like personality of the foaling mare.

In a natural herd, one birth can quickly trigger off others, suggesting that mares can not only delay their moment of labour, but also advance it slightly. For this reason it is difficult to give an accurate figure for the gestation period

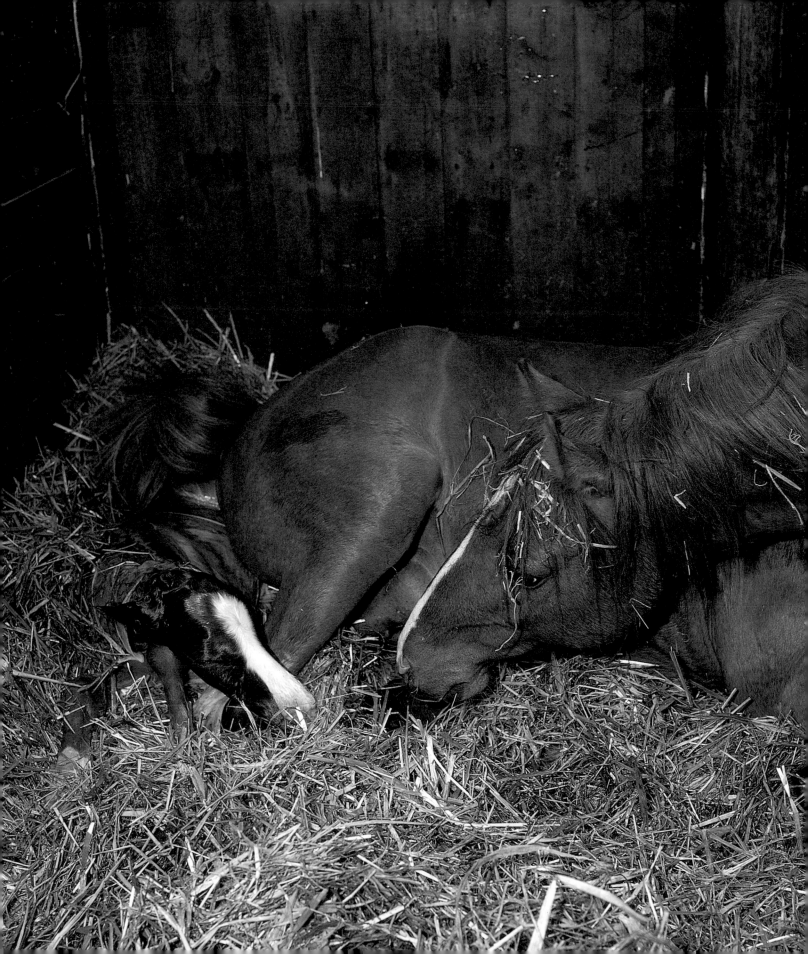

of the horse. In one wild-living group it was observed to vary from 336 days up to more than 392. (For a mare in a stable it is usually between 340 and 350 days.)

Signs that the mare is near her time include a sudden turning of the head as if to inspect the flank region (checking no doubt the strange feelings emanating from there), pawing the ground, sweating, shifting about, lying down and then getting up again. Sometimes she may kick against her belly with her hind legs, as if irritated by the growing tension there. At last she lies down and labour begins. The birth sac appears first, like an opaque balloon, and then the increasing contractions of the abdomen burst this foetal membrane and release the fluid in which the unborn foal has been lying. The mare is fascinated by the liquid pouring from her and sniffs it with great concentration, curling back her upper lip in the *flehmen* facial expression. This indicates that she is carefully checking the odour of the fluid, an important part of becoming familiar with her new foal.

Now the front feet of the foal appear and quickly the rest of the young animal follows. The whole birth is usually over in just a few minutes. In the wild, an animal like a horse cannot afford to dwell on this process or rest too long. Any early equines that did so were easy prey and did not live to pass on their genes to later generations.

As soon as the foal has emerged into the world, its eyes wide open, it tries to raise its head. The mare bends her neck round and makes gentle contact with the little animal, nose to nose. As she does so, she gives it a soft vocal greeting – a little nickering noise – and sometimes the foal answers. The bond of attachment is beginning.

When the birth is over, after a while, the mare rises and in so doing breaks the umbilical cord and automatically separates the foal from her body. She then starts licking the young one's mouth and nose, cleaning out the nostrils and aiding respiration. The foal makes mouthing movements as she touches it, the same kind of action that it will use when seeking her nipple. This is the primary action of all newborn animals and it is not long before the foal is feeding greedily. Before this can happen, however, the mare insists on further cleansing and starts to lick and nibble the foal's wet coat, working all over its body. Impatient to rise, the tiny animal keeps trying to heave itself up, only to be pushed back down again in its mother's determined efforts to dry it and, at the same time, to become acutely familiar with its personal body fragrance. Later on this odour will permit her to identify her offspring and distinguish it from other foals, even in the dark.

Two mistakes made by over-eager humans attending an equine birth are the cutting of the cord and the rubbing

life they show (often towards their mothers) attempted mounting behaviour, at an average rate of once in five hours.

Occasionally juvenile play is directed at adults. Mares tend to drive foals away if they are not their own offspring, but stallions are surprisingly tolerant. They permit youngsters to attack them and treat their assaults with remarkable restraint, even permitting mane-biting and leg-nibbling, but as the foals begin to mature the stallions' attitude changes. They may tolerate a certain amount of rough play and frolicking from yearlings and even two-year-olds, but three-year-olds are a different matter. By that age, fighting becomes serious and playtime is over. If a young adult male starts to approach a mare in a sexual manner now, he is driven away savagely by the stallion and forced to take up a subordinate position on the outskirts of the herd. The tensions and stresses of the social hierarchy of adult equine life are now upon him.

Although three-year-old horses are fertile, their fertility will continue to increase during the next few years and they can be considered fully sexually mature when they are five. By this age, wild-living males would be attempting to control mares of their own, but would still have the older and more experienced stallions to contend with. With the passage of each year they would become more and more likely to succeed as dominant males, until eventually their strength too starts to decline. Stallions can still breed when they are in their twenties, but their fertility starts to wane after they pass through the ten-to-fifteen-year-old period of their lives.

WHAT IS THE LIFESPAN OF THE HORSE?

THE TYPICAL LIFESPAN OF A THOROUGHBRED HORSE IS twenty years. With crossbreds it is slightly longer. It is possible to produce a simple chart showing the approximate relationship between the ages of humans and horses, although this is no more than a rough guide:

AGE OF HUMAN	AGE OF HORSE
20	5
40	10
50	15
60	20
70	25
80	30
90	35

A working horse is reckoned to be old at about seventeen years, its legs usually being the first part of its body to fail. As it gets still older, grey hairs begin to appear on the face, especially around the eyes and muzzle, and there is a deepening of the hollows above the eyes. The eyelids become wrinkled and there is a looseness in the lips which tend to hang down floppily from the mouth. The back of the animal becomes more and more hollow and the gait when walking much stiffer.

Record lifespans for horses are remarkable, being so far beyond the average. The world record is sixty-two years, for an eighteenth-century horse called Old Billy that was born in 1760 and died in 1822. He was a cross-breed, employed to tow barges on the canal near Warrington in Lancashire. He was still working at the age of fifty-nine, if we are to believe the old records. To employ a horse of that age to perform physical tasks is rather like asking a man of 150 to do heavy manual labour. Old Billy was either a most exceptional individual or the records of two Old Billies have been accidentally or deliberately condensed into one, as sometimes used to happen in earlier days.

The oldest pony recorded lived in France to the age of fifty-four years and the oldest thoroughbred racehorse managed forty-two years (Tango Duke, 1935-78, in Australia). Other exceptional records include another barge horse that lived to 61 years, a hunter that managed 52 years and a farm horse that was still working at 43. One horse-owner had three horses that lived to 39, 37 and 35 years, revealing that his understanding of horse care went beyond mere luck. But these are all highly unusual cases and nobody should feel they have failed their animals if they do not attain such splendid lifespans. Twenty to twenty-five years is a good life for any horse.

HOW DO A HORSE'S TEETH SHOW ITS AGE?

THE OLD SAYING 'NEVER LOOK A GIFT-HORSE IN THE mouth' reflects the fact that it is possible to judge if a horse is old and worn-out by examining its teeth. As the horse grows, so the appearance of its teeth changes and it is easy to estimate its approximate age from the length, shape and colour of its incisors. The following guide may be used:

At birth The newborn foal has only two small incisors in the upper jaw and two in the lower jaw. These are the milk incisors and will be replaced later by the adult teeth.

At 4-6 weeks Two more incisors are added in each jaw. The first, or central, incisors are now flanked by the second, or lateral, incisors (in US, the middle incisors).

At 6 months Two more incisors are added in each jaw, outside the others. These are the third, or corner, incisors. This now gives the young horse its total number of incisors: twelve (six upper and six lower). These are still the temporary or milk teeth. They all have 'cups' – that is to say, small concavities at their tips. These little dips will disappear as the teeth are worn down, and this is one of the key factors in determining the age of a horse.

At 1 year The first incisors have lost their cups – they have been worn down to the point where the tips are smooth. The second and third incisors still retain cups.

At 1½ years Now the first and second incisors have both lost their cups and been worn smooth, but the third incisors still show cups.

At 2 years All cups have been worn down and all incisor-tips are smooth.

At 2½ years The first incisors of the milk-tooth set have been replaced by the larger permanent teeth, with cups.

At 3½ years The second incisors of the milk-tooth set have now also been replaced and also display cups.

At 4½ years All milk-teeth incisors have now been replaced with larger permanent teeth and all display cups.

At 7 years The first permanent incisors are now smooth from wear, but the others still show cups.

At 8 years The second permanent incisors are now smooth from wear as well, but the third still show cups.

At 9 years All incisors have now worn smooth. All cups have gone. On the first and second incisors there is a new feature: the dental star. This is a short dark line between where the cup used to be and the front edge of the tooth. It is the upper end of the pulp cavity, revealed externally by the wear on the tip of the tooth. Dental stars first started to show at six years of age but inconspicuously and only on the first incisors. They are now clearly visible on both first and second.

They are simply being judiciously cautious, and we should never refer to the timidity of horses as suggesting a lack of intelligence. Rather it is the intelligence of a prey species.

Another difference between us and them that is crucial when discussing horse intelligence is the presence or absence of hands. We express so many of our learning skills through our fingers and the way we literally manipulate the world around us that it is hard for us to conceive the world through the mind of an animal with blunt hooves. Inside its brain a horse may well have worked out how to solve a particular problem, but then simply lacks the hands with which to implement the solution. Sometimes the teeth and muscular lips can come to the rescue, however, and when they do they reveal to us the complex workings of the equine brain. For example, individual horses have often discovered how to open the doors to their stalls or stables and escape, or gain the company of their companions. Some find out how to lift latches, others how to remove a horizontal bar. Still others develop ways of improving their meals. One animal decided it hated dry fodder and took to pushing its hay nearer and nearer to its water bowl. It then picked up mouthfuls of dry hay and dunked them in the water bowl before eating them. In this way it used its intelligence to re-create something closer to fresh grass, its favourite food.

This was not a rigid or accidental piece of behaviour. If fresh grass itself was given, or if the dry hay was dunked before being offered to the horse, the fodder was never dunked before being eaten. If the bowl was changed for buckets of water, the dunking was shifted to these buckets. The behaviour was flexible and always aimed at the same goal – to avoid boringly dry fodder.

Tests to analyse the discrimination abilities of horses have produced some remarkable results. Given pairs of patterns to look at, such as a square versus a circle, a circle versus a semi-circle, or a triangle versus some dots, with a food reward only given for one of each of these pairs, horses learned very quickly to react to the correct one. When twenty pairs of patterns were offered, horses learned to tell them apart in every case (compared with thirteen in donkeys and ten in zebras). Their scores were always well above the 50 per cent level of chance and in some cases were 100 per cent correct. Their lowest score was as high as 73 per cent, with one difficult pair. Even more impressive was the fact that twelve months after the training session there was virtually no memory loss with nineteen out of the twenty pairs of patterns. This is better than most humans could manage and reflects the fact that in the wild it is vitally important for horses to learn and memorize many different plants in their environment –

magnetic fields, which no doubt give the horses a sense of unease when they first encounter them – rather like country-dwellers moving to a noisy city and finding it stressful after the peace of rural life. After a while, the horses adjust to the situation, damp down their responses and improve their performance, but their initial distress does appear to reveal a marked sensitivity to magnetic conditions, supporting the idea that magnetic factors may be involved in equine homing.

XXIII

HOW TERRITORIAL ARE HORSES?

SOME ANIMALS WANDER OVER A HOME RANGE without ever defending their space. Others are strictly territorial, living on a clearly defined area which they defend against unwanted intruders. The horse does not fit easily into either of these two categories. Sometimes bands of wandering horses show no defensive behaviour at all and are content to roam an extensive home range without ever attempting to drive off other horses. They may even be prepared to share watering places and grazing zones without any disputes disrupting the peace and harmony of their life. All that happens when two small herds meet is that they avoid one another and quietly go their own ways. This is what happens when there is plenty of room for all. Without the pressure of crowding, the territorial imperative is not called into action. When conditions are slightly more restrictive, then true territorial defence can be observed. If a band of horses meets another under such circumstances then a battle may ensue between the rival leaders, usually the dominant stallions. When this happens, the stallion that 'owns' the territory invariably wins and drives off the intruder. A victory in such a case does not lead to prolonged persecution of the beaten stallion – all the winner wants is to repel the enemy, not to destroy him – and once he has withdrawn, peace returns immediately.

For domestic horses kept in stables, the question of territoriality is almost irrelevant. Their world has become so condensed that all sense of home range or defended region is outside their experience. However, a pattern of behaviour called 'walking the fence' can be observed whenever a stabled horse is allowed out into a new paddock. If the paddock is unfamiliar to it, its immediate response to being released there is to set off on a 'territorial patrol' in which, by moving all around the perimeter, it learns the shape and scope of its new space. After this patrolling has been fully expressed, the horse then settles down to a quieter enjoyment of the area it has been allotted.

Even large paddocks are, however, mere miniatures of a natural territory. Wild equines, for example, have been observed to have a range of 30 to 80 square miles. In travelling between grazing, drinking and sleeping locations, they will cover as much as 16 miles a day, walking in single file and often keeping to well-worn paths that they know intimately. So for their domesticated cousins there is always going to be a lifetime of greatly reduced circumstances as far as spatial freedom is concerned. Some domestic horses react to this by giving up all hope of behaving territorially. Their world is so cramped, compared with the wild state, that they simply switch off

their territorial feelings and accept the smaller, softer life. Others resist this quiet option and may occasionally become fiercely defensive in their small paddocks. Care always has to be taken when a new horse is added to a paddock where another has been for some time. The 'owner' may suddenly unleash its pent-up territorial aggression and lash out savagely at the newcomer. Without adequate supervision by the owners such an attack may become serious. The established inhabitant, either because it is harbouring a grudge over the way it has been treated in the past, or because it feels a desperate need for a bigger territory and cannot accept an intruder on what it considers to be the central core of its world, refuses to be satisfied with the submission of its enemy and

continues to attack the victim despite its repeated attempts at appeasement. Unrestrained violence of this sort reflects the abnormal spatial conditions that most domesticated horses must endure in their proximity to man, but fortunately, when it does occur, it can usually be controlled efficiently before any serious damage is done. Only in instances where horses are being kept by novices who fail to recognize that the social world of equines involves serious competition as well as cooperation will there be major risks. Old hands will know from experience that no matter how docile a horse may have become in its relations with its rider it still remains a complex social being once it is turned out with others of its own kind and must be observed closely.

HOW DO HORSES FIGHT?

LIKE ALL INTELLIGENT ANIMALS, HORSES ATTEMPT TO settle their disputes without actually coming to blows. They rely as much as possible on threat displays. With these signals they can usually decide which is going to be the dominant member of a group of equines.

In one intensive field study it was found that only 24 per cent of disputes went beyond visual and vocal threats and mild body-pushes. This figure was based on no fewer than 1,162 separate disagreements at a water-hole. Another, quite separate investigation that looked at the way horses argued over food revealed that the corresponding figure there was 22.6 per cent – remarkably close. It is safe to say, then, that three-quarters of all horse disputes are settled without resorting to violence.

The threats given include the following: the ears are laid back, the head is lowered, the neck is extended, the rear-end of the body is moved closer to the enemy, the body is used to block the path of the enemy and the enemy is pushed with the head, neck, shoulder or body of the attacker.

As the argument becomes more heated, the horse starts to snake and nod its head, the lowered, extended neck making vigorous sideways and up-and-down movements, as though the animal were tearing at the enemy's body in a savage bite. While this is going on the mouth is open, giving a bite-threat. The tail starts to swish angrily. The front legs make threat-strikes in the direction of the opponent, or they may be stamped on the ground. Or the hind legs may kick out with a threat that unless the enemy retreats it will be given a serious contact-kick, rather than one in mid-air. Head bumps and body bumps may be given and, although these are certainly contact actions, they are not done in such a way that they become fully physical acts of aggression. Loud squeals of rage are often emitted as an embellishment of these threatening actions.

If all this fails, then the horse must finally give in to brute force. To administer this it rears up on its hind legs and strikes downwards with its front feet, squealing and biting at the enemy's neck at the same time. Or it may charge at the adversary, neck thrust forwards, and attempt to bite it as savagely as possible. These actions – striking and biting – are the signs that the horse in question is a truly dominant individual. If instead it is rather defensive and nervous at the same time as being angry, then a different kind of reaction is observed. Such a horse employs a defensive, as opposed to offensive, assault. The body is swung round rapidly to present the rear-end to the opponent. At the same moment the hind legs lash out in what can be a seriously damaging one- or two-legged kick.

WHAT IS THE DIFFERENCE BETWEEN HOT-BLOODS AND COLD-BLOODS?

THERE IS A TRADITION WITH HORSE-BREEDERS THAT sees all domesticated horses as hot-bloods, warm-bloods or cold-bloods. These three types having nothing to do with body temperatures, but with the breeding and origins of the various kinds of horses.

There are only two kinds of hot-bloods: the Arabs and the thoroughbreds. These are the fine-boned aristocrats of the equine world and are sometimes referred to as full-bloods. The name hot-blood is associated with them not only because the original stock came from the hot deserts of the Middle East and North Africa but also because they are high-spirited and quick to react. The cold-bloods, by contrast, are the work horses, mostly massive animals with a stolid, calm, placid character. They are heavy-boned,

even-tempered and are descended from the northern forest type of horse – from the tundra horse and the steppe horse. They are not cold-blooded, but they do come from the colder, more northerly climes and their stockier build suits them to the intense cold of the northern winters.

The warm-bloods, sometimes called half-breds, are crosses between the two extreme types. They are usually fine-boned animals, a characteristic they inherit from their hot-blood Arab ancestors, but are less fiery in temperament and less highly-strung. Nevertheless they are much more spirited and quick to react than their cold-blood ancestors. These warm-bloods are the modern sports horses, developed for all kinds of leisure activities.

XXVII

HOW MANY HORSE BREEDS ARE THERE?

RECENT SURVEY OF HORSE BREEDS GIVES A TOTAL OF 207 distinct examples. However, some of these may not be valid – many countries and districts have their own local names for 'breeds' that are no more than minor variations of better known forms – and there may be many more breeds that are lurking in some remote region, unrecorded. But this figure gives a rough idea of just how richly varied the world of horses is today.

Of these 207 listed breeds, 67 are ponies, 36 are working horses and 104 are sports horses. In this context, the definition of a pony is any horse that is less than 58 inches (14.2 hands) high, but height is not the only feature that distinguishes ponies from horses. Ponies are much closer to the primeval ancestors of the horse, with shorter legs in relation to the size of the body and with a sturdier build, being weight-for-weight stronger than horses. There are two breeds of small animals, although technically ponies because of their size, are more horselike in proportion. They are the ancient Caspian breed and the modern Falabella. Both of these are usually referred to as 'miniature horses' rather than ponies, to emphasize their more graceful, delicate body proportions. The Caspians, recently rediscovered on the shores of the Caspian Sea in northern Iran, look like tiny Arab horses, and it is believed that they may indeed be close to the original equine from

which the Arab horses were developed thousands of years ago. They were depicted in ancient Persian carvings dating from 2,500 years ago but had not been seen by outsiders for at least a thousand years. Remaining isolated in a small area they continued to breed true and were not tampered with, leaving them much as they were in the ancient world. Then in 1965 some were brought out to the west where they have been carefully bred and protected, a living reminder of what the forerunners of our modern thoroughbreds looked like.

The Falabella is a very different story, being a modern Argentinian breed that is essentially a much reduced Shetland pony, but with the difference that it has the slender proportions of a tiny horse. The smallest of all living horses, these diminutive animals are far too lightweight to ride and are kept purely as exotic pets. With an average height of less than 34 inches they are considerably smaller than many breeds of dogs. The tiniest adult Falabella stood only 15 inches at the shoulder, compared with 40 inches for the tallest Great Dane. The idea of a horse being able to walk underneath a dog is bizarre, but these minute equines should not be looked upon as freaks, because the ancestor of all modern horses, *Eohippus* the Dawn Horse, that lived fifty million years ago, was only 10 inches high. Today, when Falabella foals are born measuring less than

12 inches at the shoulder, we are looking at something the size of those remote ancestors.

Moving from the ponies to the working horses, we go to the other extreme. These are the giants of the horse world. Some are known to have stood at over 7 feet at the shoulder (21.1 hands) and have weighed over a ton. These were the heavy horses that gave us agricultural power in the days before the internal combustion engine started to spew its fumes on to our roads and our countryside. Today they survive as cherished relics of those quieter days, magnificent specimens appearing regularly on special occasions at country shows and fairs. Devoted enthusiasts are keeping most of the major breeds alive and interest in them is, if anything, now on the increase, so that their future even in the space age is assured.

By far the most varied group of equines today is, however, the one comprising the hundred breeds of sporting horses. Sport, whether riding, hunting, racing, show-jumping, eventing or polo, keeps the twentieth-century horse in a permanent position of prominence. As the vast urban populations of cities spread and the countryside is hemmed in more and more, rural pursuits become more fiercely defended and horsemanship perversely – in the era of the motor-car and the traffic jam – is flourishing. As an antidote to the mechanization of life it appeals not only to the equestrians themselves but also to the millions who watch them – at racetracks and show-grounds and on television. The sports horse has become more than the object of the enthusiasm and passion of devoted riders – it has become a symbol of man's intimate relationship with animals and of the green past of our rural existence. In this capacity, we may well expect to see even more breeds in the future, rather than fewer.

It is of interest to examine which countries boast the greatest variety of breeds. Russia leads the way with at least 27; Britain comes second with 19; France third with 18 and the United States and Germany next with 16 each. Italy has 10 and Poland 9. But these are minimum figures, because new breeds are being developed all the time to meet the demands of our changing environment. Nevertheless they are a guide as to which countries have been most active in creating specific breeds of horses and cherishing them right through to the late twentieth century.

XXVIII

WHY DO HORSES RUN RACES?

THIS MAY SEEM A STUPID QUESTION, BUT IT IS NOT. It is unnatural for horses to gallop at high speed over long distances. So why do they do it? We know why greyhounds race – it is to pursue the hare – but what is it that makes thoroughbreds run so fast and so far?

To understand the behaviour of modern racehorses it is necessary to examine more closely their curious lifestyle. People who only set eyes on them at the racetrack often have no idea of what a strange, spartan existence they lead. When they are not racing they spend much of their time penned up in their separate stalls. There they become frustrated. Their regular training runs do little to relieve this frustration, serving only to whet the appetite for freedom of movement.

If a novice owner innocently suggests that a racehorse might enjoy being turned out into a field, the trainer will explain that this might take the animal's mind off racing. On this basis horses race because they have been boxed up to such an extent that they have been starved of any kind of powerful physical activity and have an overload of energy just waiting to erupt. On the race-day, given their head, they take off at full tilt and run and run until they are exhausted. If this exhaustion sets in before the winning-post has been passed they are either whipped or pulled up, according to how good their chances are of winning.

Such is the explosion of muscular activity in a typical horse-race that thoroughbreds are usually not capable of racing again for days. This underlines how unnatural the pattern of their lives has become. No wild horse could survive if it was only capable of rapid fleeing every few days. But then, no wild horse would be expected to flee so far. The natural predators of wild horses – the wild dogs, wolves and big cats – would kill or give up after a much shorter chase. In effect, when our racehorses rush off eagerly along the open spaces of the racetrack they are behaving rather like school-children, cooped up all day in an unnaturally immobile condition and then let out into the playground for high-intensity activity. Just as much of the play in the playground is mindless and meaningless, so is the racing along the course by the horses. It is not so much that they are fleeing, or reliving a panic escape, but rather that they are expressing themselves physically after a long period of restraint.

Yet, despite this, there is an element of fear and panic-fleeing inherent in the horse-race. This element is underlined by two facts. First, no wild horse would ever accelerate to a full gallop without being in a state of panic-fleeing. Moderate fleeing is done at the trot, when a band of horses is retreating from something suspicious. Only when the predator has broken cover and is in hot pursuit

will a wild horse break into a top-speed gallop. So somewhere in a racehorse's mind there must be a fantasy, at least, of a pursuing killer. Second, there is the pain of the whip. As it stings the flank or rump it must be reminiscent of the scratch of a feline claw or the nip of a canine mouth. Feeling this close-proximity attack, the horse makes an extra effort to escape, and continues to do so as long as it has any strength left in its limbs.

Finally, then, racing is a combination of fleeing from invisible predators and the more basic expression of highly thwarted physical activity. It is a kind of 'vacuum' or 'overflow' activity in which vigorous, healthy young animals seek escape, not from wolves or lions but from the enforced action-poverty of their highly artificial lives.

XXIX

WHY DO SOME HORSES RUN FASTER THAN OTHERS?

WHEN THE PUNTERS STARE AT THE HORSES PARADING in the paddock before a race they are earnestly seeking some small visual clues as to which will be the fastest runner. Unfortunately, the most important part of the horse is not visible to them, for it is its heart that will make the difference between winning and losing. All modern racing horses have superb limbs and muscles and are capable of reaching high speeds. That is not where the real difference lies between one highly bred horse and another. The secret is internal and invisible, much to the relief of the bookies. For it is ultimately the efficiency of the blood system of each individual thoroughbred that will be the deciding factor between glory and ignominy.

With each race, the first quarter of a mile is run anaerobically – that is to say, with the animal consuming fuel that does not require oxygen from the blood stream. After that the horse becomes involved in aerobics and it is up to the heart and lungs to supply the necessary oxygen to the muscles. The slightest weakness in the heart of infection in the lungs and the animal will lose its race. So when the racing enthusiast declares that a great racehorse is 'all heart', his emotional metaphor has a factual basis.

The most amazing aspect of the physiology of racing is the tremendous increase in heartbeat speed, from resting to full gallop. Some authorities claim that there is an amazing tenfold increase, from 25 to 250 beats per minute. Others suggest a more modest 36 to 240, but even this means an increase of nearly seven times to a pounding heart level of four beats every second. Little wonder that thoroughbreds look so exhausted after a tough race.

Exertion like this at regular intervals is clearly not a natural phenomenon for equines, but expensive horses running valuable races are asked to do more and more and to do it more and more often. The likely result is an enlarged heart and serious health risks. What happens is that as the heart grows in size it allows no room for 'the expansion of effort' during the tension of a demanding race. It has to press harder against the surrounding tissues to do its normal work. This extra pressure tires the heart and the horse 'fades' as the race nears its end. Any punter who has placed bets regularly on 'sure things' will know this phenomenon all too well. The horse does splendidly through the early and middle stages of the race, but then suddenly appears to be moving backwards. The other horses seem to be streaking past it and accelerating to the winning-post. In reality they are all slowing down slightly as they near the limits of their physical abilities, but the horse with an inefficient heart will slow down much more dramatically, creating the false impression that the others are speeding up. If a fading horse is not rested following such a race it may suffer irreversible damage to its heart.

Another important aspect of race-winners is their gait. The symmetry with which their legs touch the ground during their galloping movements is of great significance. The ideal horse, it is said, should have legs that operate 'like the spokes of a wheel', each one making contact and taking the weight of the horse in its turn to an equal degree and for an equal time interval.

If a horse with a strong heart, a powerful chest and a symmetrical gait fails to win races then what is wrong with it? Genetics and breeding may be partly to blame, but less than most people imagine. It is generally felt that if you mate two champions you will obtain champion foals, but many pundits have paid huge prices for such foals only to be bitterly disappointed. The truth is that modern thoroughbreds are so inbred that they all possess very similar genetic constitutions and the offspring of almost any of them could turn out to be champion animals. There is some bias in favour of foals from winners, but it is only that – a bias – not a certainty.

The individual personality of the horse is significant, but it is hard to say how much of this is genetically controlled and how much is the result of the quirks of personal history. The reason we are still in the dark is because racehorses are too precious and too slow-breeding for behaviour students to be able to carry out tests on their individual psychology. However, some tests carried out with animals that are easier to handle, such as white mice, have proved that it is possible to 'create' winners by simple training methods. Small mice allowed to dominate big, tough mice (by doping the big mice to make them unusually docile for a while) soon began to believe in themselves. When pitted against big mice again (undoped this time) they won their fights with them and became the dominant animals despite their small size. This kind of training technique shows how easy it is to build confidence in any animal, simply by manipulating the way in which it performs in its social encounters. The personal history of every animal is full of little incidents of this kind, and we often do not realize how, in a fleeting moment, a young foal may acquire a feeling of personal strength and determination.

If we knew that the personality of young thoroughbreds could be 'helped' as they mature, we might be able to enhance their stubborn resolve to go on and on running even when the exertion has started to cause them the sort of physical discomfort that human athletes know so well. To understand this determination a little better it is worth looking at the way in which a wild herd of horses flees from trouble. The safest place to be if you are an escaping ungulate, whether a horse, a deer or an antelope, is in the middle of the herd as it runs away from danger. It is the stragglers that get picked off by predators, and sometimes the front-runners, too. The front-runners, if they go too far ahead of the herd, become just as isolated as the stragglers bringing up the rear, and then they too fall prey to lurking killers – the ones waiting in ambush. So the natural urge of a galloping horse must be to keep with the group; in other words, there is safety in numbers. Translate this into racing terms and you have the typical race-winner. If you run films of races backwards you see the way in which, nearly always, the winner lies in 'midfield' until the last stretch of the race. Frequently it is in third or fourth place, a good position from which to make the last bid for the front. Up to that point, it has felt safe and would probably stay there if it were not for the urging of its jockey. But with the winning-post coming close, he drives it on, frequently using the whip to simulate the stinging lash of a predator's claws raking the fleeing animal's rump. This extra stimulus makes the horse surge forwards and it passes its companions to win. At the point where it throws caution to the wind and takes up the 'front-runner position' its natural fear of getting too far in front of the herd, and thereby becoming a potential victim for predators hiding in ambush, is overcome by the 'certainty' that there is a killer, slashing at its rear-end.

Needless to say, rival jockeys are also whipping their horses at this point, if there is a chance of them winning. So the last furlong is a test of stamina, as each competing

horse struggles to escape the 'attack' from the rear. And stamina, at the end of a long race, comes back to the question of heart — both literally in terms of blood circulation, and metaphorically in terms of individual personality.

Some champion horses do not need this last-ditch encouragement. They take the lead not so much because they abandon the security of the group but simply because the group is starting to lag behind. They have good 'race-rhythm', in that they do not race ahead too soon and have to be held back — which wastes precious energy — and they do not lag behind early on and have to be driven hard far too soon. Either way the uneven pace would inevitably consume extra energy. The perfect rhythm is one in which the animal always keeps up steadily with the main body of horses until the final phase when, in racing parlance, the jockey can 'press the button' if he needs to and the horse, at his urging, will surge forwards with a powerful final run-in.

WHY DO SOME HORSES
RUN SLOWER THAN OTHERS?

AFTER EVERY RACE A LITTLE RITUAL IS PERFORMED between the owner, trainer and jockey of each of the losing horses. This is the 'Why we were beaten' ceremony and involves the search for an excuse that will persuade the owner to pay next month's training bills instead of selling off his disappointing horse.

The simple truth is taboo during this ritual. The most obvious comments may not be uttered: that the horse is no good; that the other horses were better; that the jockey rode badly; or that the trainer failed to prepare the horse. It is also forbidden to mention the fact that horses are not machines but living beings susceptible to occasional inconsistencies in their behaviour. The astronomical cost of keeping a modern racehorse in training is such that the animal is required to be nothing short of a consistent winner . . . without some very good and very particular reason. This is where the inventiveness of the trainer and jockey are called into play. The same excuse will not do after each lost race. New reasons have to be found.

When one exasperated owner wrote to *Sporting Life* giving some of the bizarre excuses he had been offered over the years, the paper was soon flooded with additional examples from other frustrated owners. Here is a modified and simplified selection of them with some additional ones collected personally. The top fifty are:

1 The horse swallowed its tongue. **2** The horse stepped in a rabbit-hole on the far side of the track. **3** The horse was hit by a flying divot. **4** The horse swallowed a flying divot. **5** The horse disliked the tight bends. **6** The horse was stung by an insect down at the start. **7** The horse was distracted by a television van. **8** The horse did not like the rain. **9** The horse had an abscess in its mouth. **10** The horse had a sore foot. **11** The horse did not want to go past the racehorse stables. **12** The horse suffered from muscle spasms. **13** The horse did not like the high winds. **14** The horse was lazy/was too keen. **15** The horse was bumped during the race. **16** The horse was kicked during the race. **17** The horse disliked the slow pace/disliked the fast pace. **18** The horse jumped too carefully/over-jumped. **19** The horse felt crowded in the large field of runners. **20** The horse missed the competition in the very small field of runners. **21** The horse did not act on the hard going/did not act on the soft going. **22** The horse hated the left-handed track/hated the right-handed track. **23** The horse was under-worked/was over-worked. **24** The horse would improve over a shorter distance/needs a longer trip. **25** The horse missed the start and then had too much to do. **26** The horse was struck in the face by a rival jockey's whip. **27** The horse's saddle was slipping/was too tight and was pinching. **28** The horse was

too inexperienced/was too experienced. **29** The horse bolted on the way to the start/bolted at the off. **30** The horse was hemmed in and could not find a gap. **31** The horse travelled badly during the long journey to the racetrack. **32** The horse suffered from exhaust fumes inside the horse-box. **33** The horse had been upset by a fireworks display near the stables the night before. **34** The horse's girth-strap broke. **35** The horse lost a plate. **36** The horse had come into season. **37** The horse hit the front too soon/needs to be a front-runner. **38** The horse was off its feed. **39** The horse needed the run-out. **40** The horse should not be whipped/needs stronger handling. **41** The horse needs castrating. **42** The horse may have a low blood count. **43** The horse's champion sire did not reach peak form until he was much older. **44** The jockey thought there was another lap/thought there wasn't another lap. **45** The jockey mistakenly thought something was wrong and pulled the horse up. **46** The jockey dropped his whip. **47** The jockey mistook the last furlong post for the winning-post and eased off. **48** The jockey was kicked during the race. **49** The handicapper had been too severe and the horse was carrying too much weight. **50** The stable has a virus.

Any racehorse-owner who has not found himself confronted with one of these many excuses from a trainer or jockey after a race must possess a miracle horse.

Perhaps the most spectacular excuse for a horse doing badly in a race was that offered by an apprentice jockey who had been hauled up before the stewards to explain his appalling ride. Asked why he had not done better he replied, 'Because the gov'nor told me in no circumstances was I to finish in the first six.'

WHY DO RACEHORSES
NOT RUN FASTER EACH YEAR?

WITH EACH NEW SEASON HUMAN ATHLETES SEEM TO run faster, breaking records in almost every event. On the human racetrack hardly any record is more than a few years old. But as the records show with thoroughbred racehorses, the scene is very different. Despite careful breeding plans and the investment of huge sums of money by the owners, the modern racehorse appears to have come to the end of its line, in terms of speed. Records are broken only rarely and in general there has been little improvement over the past century. Why should this be? Why is it that generation after generation of selective breeding, always favouring the fastest horses, has not led to gradual improvement? Something is clearly amiss. Racing is an ancient sport. In its earliest form, the horses were not ridden. Rival desert chieftains kept their horses thirsty and then released them at a set distance from a watering-place. The first animal to reach the water and drink was the winner. The earliest detailed records of a racehorse trainer date from 3,338 years ago in the Middle East. A little later, in ancient Greece, the first mounted horse-races were begun 2,636 years ago. The horses were ridden bareback. About 150 years later special races for mares and for young apprentice riders were introduced. The Romans became racing fanatics and 1,900 years ago there were as many as a hundred races a day. Heavy gambling, vast crowds of spectators, riots, race fixing, bribery, horse doping and all the other traditional elements of the horse-race scene were already much in evidence. But this was not to last. With the fall of the Roman Empire organized horse-racing vanished. The supply of fast oriental horses dried up and the heavier warhorses and working horses came to dominate the scene.

A thousand years passed and then the Middle East exerted its equine influence once more. Crusaders marvelled at the swift horses of their enemies and could not resist bringing some back with them when they returned to their European homes. About eight hundred years ago there were weekly races in London, using these speedy imported animals, and the first recorded racing-purse was offered to the winner of one such race. The prize was forty gold pounds, a huge sum in those days. But racing did not gain a strong foothold. It remained a minor diversion, with hunting horses and warhorses considered far more important. Only when fast cavalry replaced the heavy horses of the armoured knights did equine speed reassert itself as a significant preoccupation. As the centuries passed racing became more and more organized until the stage was set for the birth of modern thoroughbred racing.

The fact is that a light flick of the whip is no more cruel than slapping your own thigh, and with an animal as sensitive as the horse it does the job just as well as the infliction of pain.

If the solution is this easy, why then is there a problem? The answer lies in the enormous pressures that are put upon jockeys to win important races. If the owners of their mounts see them lose a race by a short distance without lashing at their horses' rumps, they are liable to accuse the jockeys of not trying hard enough. Gamblers at risk of losing large sums of money can be heard bellowing 'Hit him, hit him!' as their chosen horse comes thundering in a close second. It is not that these are particularly cruel men, but the racing fever that possesses them in the final seconds of a race drives them considerably beyond their normal restraints. And this is precisely what happens to some jockeys. They feel that if only they could encourage

the horse a little more it could find that extra speed and race past its opponents to finish first. So instead of flicking the whip, they start lashing the horse as hard as they can, trying to drive it on. It is this that certain sections of the public have come to hate and which turns them against the world of horse-racing.

Severe whipping of this kind is far less successful in speeding up a racehorse than these lashing jockeys imagine. Although a touch on the rump gives the horse the idea that there may be a killer striking out at it from behind, and can make it speed up, a really savage blow there can do something else. It can make the horse swerve away from the source of pain. Since the whip always lands on one side or the other of the horse's body this can mean a sudden sideways lurch that can disrupt the animal's rhythm and actually slow it down for a vital split second. So there is no excuse for violent whipping under any circumstances.

WHY DO WE SPEAK OF STEEPLECHASING?

WE OWE STEEPLECHASING TO THE CUNNING OF THE fox and the dishonesty of humans. The fox enters the story one afternoon in the middle of the eighteenth century when a frustrated group of fox-hunters were returning home from a disappointing day's sport. Their chase had been fruitless and not a single fox had been caught. To salvage something from the occasion one of the hunters is said to have issued a challenge on the spur of the moment, wagering that he could reach the clearly visible steeple of the home village first. The object of the race was to make straight for it, regardless of what obstacles were in the way, and touch it with the whip to be declared the winner. Thus was born the jump-racing which to this day we call by its original eighteenth-century name of steeplechasing.

Before this event occurred there had been a long tradition of both flat-racing and hunting, but for some reason nobody had been inventive enough to combine the two. Now they were put together and the new sport quickly gained support. The very first recorded steeple-chase took place in Ireland in 1752 when a Mr O'Callaghan and a Mr Blake raced over 4½ miles starting at Buttevant church and ending at St Leger church. It is recorded that the prize was a 'hogshead of claret, a pipe of port, and a quarter-cask of Jamaica rum'. It is not, however, recorded who won the contest. Presumably after enjoying the prize no one was in a fit state to record anything.

Dishonest humans enter the story a little later, in 1810 to be precise. Throughout the second half of the eighteenth century steeplechasing, from church to church (or point-to-point, as the saying went), continued to flourish in an informal way, but then at the start of the nineteenth century progressed to the status of a more serious, organized sport. The reason had to do with skulduggery among flat-racers. Certain flat-races were for hunting horses – horses that were genuinely ridden on the hunting field and were not specifically bred for racing. Some riders pretended that their mounts were hunters when in reality they were speedy thoroughbreds. They entered them in hunter races and easily beat the heavier, slower jumping horses developed for the tougher pursuit of cross-country running and leaping. To defeat them someone suggested adapting for the formal racetrack the crude steeplechasing that was taking place across natural countryside.

The first true steeplechase took place at Bedford over a 3-mile course on which eight fences had been built. The obstacles were made severe enough to defeat any flat-racing horse inexperienced at cross-country jumping. They were 4½ feet high with a strong bar across the top. The

witnessing today when, in a spectacular parade, show or fair, the heavy horses are displayed wearing their heavy trappings festooned with glittering horse-brasses. Nobody may be aware of what this is really about, not even the horse-owners themselves. Superficially, it has become no more than an appealingly decorative event, but beneath the surface it is a pagan spectacle.

Looking at the individual designs, it is clear that the simple, plain sun disk is the primary form and this is still used today in pride of place on the horse's forehead, where it is known as the 'Sunflash'. It is called this because it flashes gold in the sun as the animal moves. This is an important quality of all horse-brasses and the reason why they were polished so ardently in earlier times is that by glittering in the sun they were thought to dazzle the Evil Eye and in this way repel it even more successfully. Dull trappings were considered to be far less effective.

In addition to the circular sun disk, there was also the rayed-sun or sunburst. Other ancient emblems included swastikas (symbols of the sun moving through the heavens), moons, stars, wheels, hearts (borrowed from

ancient Egypt), sacred hands, horns, acorns, birds, beasts and flowers, especially the lotus-flower (another Egyptian motif). These were the earliest images, but in Victorian times there was a sudden rush to increase the number of patterns and before long there were literally hundreds to choose from, although the designs of the new ones owed little to their pagan roots. Now, almost anything that took the Victorians' fancy was included and earlier traditions were gradually forgotten. It has been estimated that there were no fewer than seven hundred different figures portrayed and a thousand abstract patterns. Some authorities put the total as high as three thousand different designs – a challenge for any obsessive collector. Since 1820 the hammered brasses have been replaced by cast ones and in recent times these have been mass-produced, not for horses but for sale directly to enthusiasts without them ever being used. There is an irony in the fact that the amulets intended to protect the draught-horse from destruction have outlived it. They were clearly not effective against those staring Evil Eyes of the twentieth century, the headlights of the motor car.

XXXVIII

WHY DO WE NOT EAT HORSES?

HORSEFLESH IS HIGHLY NUTRITIOUS AND BY ALL accounts tastes good, so why is there such a powerful taboo against eating it? This taboo is not, as some may imagine, a modern development of horse-loving nations, with people becoming increasingly sensitive about eating their animal companions. It has a much more ancient and more obscure origin. Over a thousand years ago, for example, the subject was taken seriously enough for the Pope to issue an order totally prohibiting the eating of horseflesh under any circumstances.

To understand how this came about we have to look back to the beginning of man's relationship with the horse. We know from the bones found in Ice Age cave dwellings that our early ancestors hunted and ate horses. The favoured method of hunting was to make a herd of wild horses panic and fall over the edge of a cliff. This crude technique was refined as the hunting of the Old Stone Age gave way to the farming of the New Stone Age. Now groups of wild horses were rounded up and kept under human control. As domestication progressed, additional uses were found for the horse. Although still mainly kept as a source of meat, it also provided tough hides for clothing and for covering simple shelters, mare's milk for drinking, and bone and hoof for implements and ornaments.

Such exploitation was never taken to extremes, however, as it was with certain other domestic animals such as cattle. There was no equine equivalent of the heavy-bodied beef cattle or the large-uddered milk cattle. The early horses stayed much as they had always been. The reason for this was that, from about five thousand years ago right up to the present day, the horse has had one dominant role in human life – that of a beast of burden, a means of transporting first human belongings and then human beings themselves.

The laden or ridden horse transformed human life in a dramatic way. Hitherto undreamed-of mobility and warfare of a deadly kind was now possible. The horse, in short, was becoming the most important animal known to man. Little wonder that legends were woven around it and that it became increasingly revered and eventually even sacred. For superstitious people it became clear that only such a marvellous animal as the horse was fit for the gods. Only the horse could carry the gods through the skies and this explained the frightening (and, in early days, inexplicable) sounds of thunder and lightning. They were, it was fervently believed, the roar of the heavenly hooves and the crack of the heavenly whip.

Because of its association with powerful deities, the horse inevitably became an important sacrificial animal in many of the earlier pagan religions. Believers gained strength by eating its flesh and drinking its blood. And it is this that is the key to the later taboo on devouring horseflesh. For when christianity began to spread and gain momentum, it mounted a campaign of new rules which discredited the sacred customs of the old religions. In this way the devouring of horseflesh became wicked and dirty.

In some areas this reduction of the horse's role from sacred being to mere beast of burden was difficult to achieve, and horse-eating continued despite the urgings of the Christian church. That is why, in A.D. 732, Pope Gregory III was forced to lay down the papal law on this subject. The Celts, with their special goddess of horses called Epona, were so stubbornly resistant to the new Christian dictum that even as late as the twelfth century an Irish king was required, at his inauguration, to take a bath in horse soup. A white mare was ritually slaughtered, butchered and boiled to make a broth. The new king then sat in the broth, ate pieces of horseflesh and literally drank his own bath water.

Pagan horse-eating persisted here and there for several more centuries but eventually died out almost entirely throughout the Christian world. Other major religions were also opposed to it. Buddha specifically prohibited it. Mohammed never ate horseflesh and, although he never outlawed it, few Moslems today will touch it. The same is true for Hindus.

As a result of these widespread religious restrictions, horse-eating has become a very rare practice in today's world. It surfaced only as a much maligned practice of the starving and those suffering from extreme poverty. Battlefields strewn with the carcasses of valiant warhorses were too rich in precious protein to be ignored by wartorn peasants. But there was always unease about such scavenging. This unease has lasted right down to the present day, with a blanket of silence being thrown over the disposal of the bodies of dead horses. If they are to be eaten, they are often exported first, to hide the deed, or they are consigned to the anonymity of the pet-food trade.

There was one remarkable attempt to revive horse-eating in Europe, but it failed miserably. Surprisingly it came in the middle of the last century at a time when the Victorians were at their most sentimental about animals. It was caused by official concern over the bad diet of the poorer classes. Since many people were suffering from serious malnutrition, the enormous waste of good horseflesh that was common at the time was viewed as unacceptable and serious attempts were made to glamorize this freely available but scorned source of meat. In 1868 a special society was formed in England called 'The Society for the Propagation of Horse Flesh as an Article of Food'. An amazing and much publicized dinner was held at the august Langham Hotel in London. The menu included the following items among its nine courses:

Horse soup; fillet of sole in horse-oil; terrine of lean horse-liver; fillet of roast Pegasus; turkey with horse-chestnuts; sirloin of horse stuffed with Centaur; braised rump of horse; chicken garnished with horse-talons; gladiator's rissoles; tongue of Trojan horse; lobster in old-hack-oil; and jellied horses' hooves in Maraschino. There was also a buffet of collared horse-head, baron of horse and boiled withers.

The sober, economic side of this curious propaganda was that widespread epidemics had cut a swathe through the cattle population and beef prices had soared. If horses – then numbered in their millions as a means of transport – could have been exploited at the end of their trotting days, an immensely valuable new meat supply would have become available – if only people could have been weaned on to this new (or, to be more correct, ancient) form of food. But they could not. Pockets of acceptance were established in some countries, especially France and Belgium with their *chevaline* enthusiasts, but in general the attempt was a failure. The magazine *Punch* summed it up by giving two definitions: *hippophagy* – the eating of horseflesh; *hypocrisy* – saying horseflesh is very good.

A Cambridge don, in an attempt to avoid assailing the nobility of the horse, turned his attentions to the more humble donkey. He had a nine-year old animal fattened

and butchered for the Master's table at Trinity College, but the idea never caught on. Its failure was aided by Oxford dons who were quick to remark that for the head of a Cambridge college to devour an old donkey was tantamount to cannibalism.

The church, perhaps because it had forgotten all about Celtic horse-goddesses and the religious roots of the horseflesh taboo, was silent about these Victorian attempts to reintroduce horsemeat to the human menu. The failure was due instead to a new attitude towards animal life. Darwin had shown that human beings are related to other species and a stronger 'fellow-feeling' was growing. With it came animal welfare organizations and widespread opposition to animal cruelty. Vegetarianism was becoming an organized movement for the first time. People were generally less bloodthirsty where animals were concerned. At Holy Communion they still drank the blood of Christ and ate his flesh, in a sanitized Christian adaptation of the earlier pagan feasts where the blood and flesh of sacred horses were consumed, but the blood was now cheap wine and the flesh was no more than thin wafers of biscuit.

The new mood was one in which only animals whose sole purpose on the farm was to provide food were acceptable on the menu. Any other domestic animals were taboo because we had a different kind of contract with them. Horses, dogs and cats were our servants and our companions and were not for eating. If an old horse had given its life to supporting us on its back, then it deserved some reward at the end of its working life. Homes for retired horses suddenly seemed more appropriate than the knacker's yard. And so it has remained, with the new sensitivity maintaining the ancient taboo, but for very different reasons.

WHAT IS HORSEPOWER?

FOR MANY YEARS MOTOR-CARS AND OTHER FORMS OF engine were given horsepower values to indicate their strength. It was fondly and not unreasonably believed by most car-owners that an 8 hp car was as powerful as eight horses. This was not, however, the case.

The idea of using horsepower as a measure of the strength of engines was conceived by the Scottish engineer James Watt as a way of making his new-fangled steam engines more understandable. In the eighteenth century people were used to thinking in terms of the work rate of horses and so this provided a familiar grading system for the new machinery.

In order to calculate the power of a horse, Watt went to the London breweries where strong dray horses were toiling and carried out a series of measurements, arriving at a figure which he thought represented a fair average. This was the true horsepower, but for some strange reason he decided to multiply it by 1.5 to produce his official figure for the power of one horse, which was 33,000 foot-pounds per minute (or the power needed to shift 33,000 pounds a distance of one foot in one minute). He did this, it is said, 'in order to rate his steam engines conservatively in terms of horsepower.' In other words, to be 10 hp an engine had to have the power of fifteen muscular dray horses. This curious decision was the opposite of bragging and was presumably intended to make the actual strength of his machines surprising rather than disappointing after mental comparison with a team of horses.

From the very beginning his horsepower system came under attack. It was described as 'a new and shockingly unscientific unit . . . insensibly coming into use.' Despite this it remained in popular use for many years because people could easily equate the power of their motor-car with the power of a team of horses pulling them along. It gave early motor-cars an image of massive strength which made up for their many faults and drawbacks.

WHY DO WE CALL
PROFESSIONAL RIDERS JOCKEYS?

IN EARLIER CENTURIES THE NAME JACK WAS USED AS a general term for any unidentified man 'of the common people'. In Scotland, peasants were given the same familiar name, but with the slightly different pronunciation: Jock. The juvenile version of Jock, applied especially to lads working as grooms, was Jockie. By the early seventeenth century this term was widely applied to young horse-dealers. These young professional horse-handlers provided the original source from which the first hired riders were drawn for racing. By the late seventeenth century the word jockey had come into being as the name for any professional rider and has remained with us ever since in this role. So, in origin at least, a jockey is a young Scottish peasant.

This is the generally accepted source of the word, but there is one voice of dissent. A Victorian expert insisted that 'the word Jockey is neither more nor less than the term *chukni* slightly modified, by which the gypsies designate the formidable whips which they usually carry, and which are at present in general use among horse-traffickers under the title of jockey-whips.' Other scholars refer to this idea as 'mere fancy', but it may have played a secondary role in fixing the name.

It has certainly remained well fixed, for it has spread to many other languages including French, Spanish, Portuguese and German. Incidentally, the familiar jockey's cap was borrowed from an ancient Roman design developed for charioteers. They wore a bronze version that protected their skulls from damage and which bore a peak that shielded their eyes from the often dazzling sun. The same design was borrowed for English schoolboys' caps.

XLI

WHY IS A HORSE CALLED A HORSE?

MOST OF US USE NAMES LIKE 'HORSE', 'PONY', 'stallion', 'mare', and 'foal' without ever considering where they came from. They are simply part of the language and we leave it at that. But if we look closer at the origins of these terms, some intriguing facts come to light that would be unheard of by the average person.

HORSE

Experts still argue about the origin of this word, but the favourite theory is that in ancient times a similar term meant 'swift' or 'running' and that our modern name has grown out of that definition. This seems reasonable enough when it is recalled that increased mobility for human horse-owners was the primary advantage in the domestication of this species.

PONY

Today we use the name pony for a small horse which is not more than 58 inches (14.2 hands) high, regardless of age or sex, but it has not always been associated with this meaning. It started out as the Latin word *pullus*, meaning a foal. From this developed the word *pullanus*, meaning a colt. In Old French this became transformed into *poulain*, and a small colt was given the special title of *poulenet*.

When it reached Scotland, this word (pronounced 'pool-ney') was modified to *powney* (pronounced 'poo-ney') by dropping the 'l'. There it became strongly associated with the tiny Scottish horses found in the Shetlands and elsewhere. About two hundred years ago, dictionaries referred to ponies as 'little Scotch horses', so it seems that we owe our modern term to the Scots, 'poo-ney' evolving to become 'po-ny' in pronunciation as it travelled back south of the border.

STALLION

An adult male horse that has not been castrated has been called a stallion since the fourteenth century. It means literally 'one kept in a stall' – the 'stall-i-on' – and it was applied to an entire male horse because such an animal was housed in a separate compartment, or stall, due to its boisterous nature. The term appears to have originated in Italy, where there was an early word *stallione* from which our modern name has descended.

MARE

This is an Anglo-Saxon name in origin. The Anglo Saxon word for horses in general was *mearh* and the feminine of this was *mere*, from which we obtained the modern mare for an adult female horse.

FOAL

From the time of its birth until it has been weaned any young horse is known as a foal. This comes from its Anglo-Saxon name, *fola*. The corresponding feminine is *filly*, and we still use this term today for any young female horse, from the time it is weaned until it is four years old.

COLT

The name colt, which today signifies a weaned male horse until it is four years old, has not always had this narrow meaning. For example, it is found in the seventeenth-century translation of the book of Genesis, where there is a reference to 'thirty camels with their colts'. Another Biblical mention describes a colt as 'the foal of an ass'. Clearly the term was not originally intended to refer specifically to young male equines, but to young animals of a much more general kind. Also, it was at first applied to both sexes, and one could speak of a 'female colt'. But as time passed it became confined more and more to young male equines and today is solely applied to them.

GELDING

When a colt is sexually mature it either becomes a sexually active stallion or is castrated and becomes a gelding. The word *geld* is an old Scandinavian term meaning 'barren', hence a gelding is 'one who is made barren'.

BRONCO

In Western movies we often hear a cowboy reference to a 'bucking bronco'. This is due to Mexican influence, the name *bronco* coming from an old Spanish word for something rough – the bronco was originally a half-broken horse that was rough to handle.

HACK

This name, referring to a horse that is for hire or used for simple riding work, comes to us from France. The French word *haquene[ac]e* meant a horse that only ambled along and was used largely by ladies. This type of animal was often employed to pull coaches and was frequently over-worked and over-used, hence our terms a 'hackneyed phrase' and 'a hack writer'. It was usually a horse of only moderate quality, not suited to hunting, war or other more specialized activities.

THOROUGHBRED

This is the term we use today for a horse with a pedigree – one with the names of its sire and dam in the General Stud Book. Originally such an animal was known simply as a 'bred-horse' and was contrasted with a 'cocktail' (a contraction of 'a cock-tailed horse'), meaning an equine with a docked tail that stood up like the tail of a cockerel. Horses employed for hunting or pulling coaches were the ones that were most likely to have their tails docked in this way and these were also the horses least likely to have a pedigree, hence the connection between cocktails and non-thoroughbreds. This old equestrian term has given rise to our modern-day name for a mixed drink. Because the horse had mixed parentage and the drink has mixed ingredients we have called the latter after the former. So, when we drink a cocktail today we are silently paying homage to a mongrel horse with a tail like a cock.

WHY DO WE CALL A
BAD DREAM A NIGHTMARE?

IF WE CALLED A BAD DREAM A NIGHTFRIGHT IT WOULD BE easy to understand, but why a night*mare*? What does it have to do with a female horse?

Very little, is the short answer. In this context, the word mare comes from the Anglo-Saxon and means evil spirit or incubus. The incubus was an unpleasant demon who visited sleeping women and sat on their chests, nearly suffocating them. More specifically he was a demon lover who ravished his victims as they twitched and choked in agonized slumber. The resultant offspring, it was said, were often misshapen. Witches welcomed him, innocent girls dreaded him. Viewed with a more objective, practical, modern eye, his exploits doubtless helped to explain embarrassing pregnancies or justified the disposal of deformed babies.

Nocturnal writhings and dreams of erotic assault, caused by intense sexual frustration, could also be explained away as reactions to his unwanted attentions. The sexual nature of nightmares was understood long ago. Writing in 1621 Robert Burton commented, 'Maids and widows were particularly subject to terrible dreams in the night, a symptom of melancholy which can be cured by marriage.'

The confusion of the demon 'mare' with the female-horse 'mare' seems to stem from paintings produced two hundred years ago by the Swiss artist Fuseli. They show a sleeping woman with a demon squatting on her chest while through her bedroom curtains there peers the head of a sinister blind horse. The paintings are entitled *Nightmare*. In their day the Fuseli pictures became famous and were produced endlessly as etchings. The staring, blind horse became the 'mare' of the nightmare. Whether this was Fuseli merely playing with words or whether he had a more complicated idea behind his imagery is hard to say, but art critics have assumed the latter. Said one, 'The horse with its phosphorescent eyes may be the "mare" on which the incubus rides through the air, apart from being a timeless symbol of virile sexuality.'

This misleading association seems to have led to the idea that people suffering from bad dreams are being haunted by horrific, nocturnal demon-horses, when in reality the equine connection is irrelevant.

WHY ARE HORSES OFTEN SAID TO BE HAG-RIDDEN?

IN EARLIER TIMES WHEN MANY SUPERSTITIONS surrounded the keeping of horses, it was often feared they might fall prey to the attentions of witches. These evil women, it was believed, entered the stables during the night and stole the horses to ride away to their secret coven meetings. The old hags rode them so far and so furiously through the night that they completely exhausted them. By the time they returned them to their stalls – just before dawn – the animals were covered in sweat and suffering from breathing difficulties. Found like this by the stablemen in the morning, there was no doubt what had happened and some unfortunate old woman living near by would soon find herself persecuted yet again. It was easy to lay the blame against evil forces in this way and to explain the poor condition of the horses as the result of being 'hag-ridden', but there was, of course, a much simpler explanation. Early stables were often poorly designed. Security was given precedence over health, and the compartments were frequently designed without any windows. After a long night shut up in the stagnant air, with a serious lack of oxygen, the wretched animals were found in the morning to be drained of energy and bathed in sweat. The wickedness of witches was in reality the stupidity of the stablemen.

ACKNOWLEDGEMENTS

The publishers thank the following photographers and organisations for their kind permission
to reproduce photographs in this book:

1 Oxford Scientific Films/Renee Lynn; 2 Oxford Scientific Films/Philip Tull; 3 DIAF/Bernard Régent; 6 Oxford Scientific Films/Martyn Chillmaid; 8 NHPA/Christophe Ratier; 9 Bruce Coleman/Geoff Dore; 10 Bruce Coleman/Fritz Prenzel; 11 Oxford Scientific Films/Alan & Sandy Carey; 12-13 RSPCA Photo Library/E.A. Janes; 14 Oxford Scientific Films/Mark Burnett; 15 Oxford Scientific Films/Philip Tull; 16 Animals Animals/Henry Ausloos; 18 G. Boiselle; 19 Kit Houghton; 20 Zefa; 22 DIAF/Henry Ausloos; 23 DIAF/Erwan Quemere; 24 Kit Houghton; 25 DIAF/Alain Le Bot; 26 Jacana/Frédéric; 28 Bruce Coleman/Dr Eckart Pott; 29 Jacana/Frédéric; 30 Animals Animals/Henry Ausloos; 31 Kit Houghton; 33 G. Boiselle; 34 Zefa; 36 RSPCA Photo Library/D. Muscroft; 37 NHPA/Agence Nature; 39 Animals Animals/Henry Ausloos; 40 Zefa; 42 Oxford Scientific Films/Philip Tull; 43 Oxford Scientific Films/David Thompson; 44 above Oxford Scientific Films/Okapia/Robert Maier; 44 below Animals Animals/David M. Barron; 46 NHPA/Stephen Dalton; 47 Bruce Coleman/Jane Burton; 48 Jacana/Guy Thouvenin; 49 Bruce Coleman/Hans Reinhard; 50 Animals Animals/Barbara J. Wright; 51 G. Boiselle; 52 Animals Animals/Renee Stockdale; 53 Jacana/Frédéric; 54-5 NHPA/Alberto Nardi; 56 G. Boiselle; 58 NHPA/Henry Ausloos; 59 Oxford Scientific Films/Konrad Wothe; 60-61 Kit Houghton; 62 Kit Houghton; 63 Bruce Coleman/Jane Burton; 64 Animals Animals/Barbara J. Wright; 65 above G. Boiselle; 65 below Animals Animals/Francis Lepine; 66 NHPA/Henry Ausloos; 68 DIAF/Jean-Yves Ferret; 69 G. Boiselle; 71 Bruce Coleman/Jane Burton; 72 RSPCA Photo Library/Mark Hamblin; 73 Animals Animals/Ralph A. Reinhold; 74 Oxford Scientific Films/Animals Animals/Henry R. Fox; 76 Bruce Coleman/Jane Burton; 77 Oxford Scientific Films/Philip Tull; 78 Animals Animals/Barbara J. Wright; 80-81 DIAF Marc Grenet; 82 Kit Houghton; 83 Animals Animals/Sydney Thomson; 84 Animals Animals/Carol L. Geake; 86 Animals Animals/Renee Stockdale; 87 Animals Animals/Robert Pearcey; 90 Bruce Coleman/Hans Reinhold; 91 Animals Animals/Charlie Palek; 92 Kit Houghton; 93 Bruce Coleman/Eric Crichton; 95 Jacana/H.I. Rodriguez; 96 Zefa; 97 NHPA/Henry Ausloos; 98 The Image Bank/Stefano Scata; 99 Oxford Scientific Films/Photo Researchers/Jerry Irwin; 100 Oxford Scientific Films/Philip Tull; 101 Animals Animals/Robert Pearcey; 102-3 G. Boiselle; 104 Animals Animals/Barbara J. Wright; 105 Animals Animals/Barbara J. Wright; 107 Tony Stone Images/Thomas Zimmerman; 108 above Tony Stone Images; 108 below The Image Bank; 111 Colorsport; 113 The Image Bank/Yellow Dog Productions; 115 Tony Stone Images/Thomas Zimmerman; 118 Colorsport/Piran; 119 Colorsport; 121 Colorsport; 122-3 Colorsport; 124-6 Kit Houghton; 128 The Image Bank/Daniel Arsenault; 130 RSPCA Photo Library/Dorothy Burrows; 131 Zefa; 134 Agence Top/M. Fraudreau; 135 Zefa; 137 Tony Stone Images; 138 NHPA/Henry Ausloos; 139 Bruce Coleman/Fritz Prenzel; 141 Oxford Scientific Films/Terry Heathcote.

The line illustrations, throughout are reproduced by courtesy of Dover Publications.

By the same author

The Biology of Art
The Mammals
Men and Snakes (co-author)
Men and Apes (co-author)
Men and Pandas (co-author)
Zootime
Primate Ethology (editor)
The Naked Ape
The Human Zoo
Patterns of Reproductive Behaviour
Intimate Behaviour
Manwatching

Gestures (co-author)
Animal Days
The Soccer Tribe
Inrock
The Book of Ages
The Art of Ancient Cyprus
Bodywatching
The Illustrated Naked Ape
Catwatching
The Secret Surrealist
Catlore

Dogwatching
The Animals Roadshow
The Human Nestbuilders
Horsewatching
The Animal Contract
Animalwatching
Babywatching
Christmas Watching
The World of Animals
The Human Animal
Bodytalk
Catworld

040-907